SPEAK UP

SPEAK UP

THE PUBLIC SPEAKING PRIMER

BY CAROL ROAN

Press 53
Winston-Salem, North Carolina

Press 53
PO Box 30314
Winston-Salem, NC 27130

First Edition

Copyright © 2010 by Carol Roan

Original edition published © 1995 as *Speak Easy: A Guide to Successful Performances, Presentations, Speeches, and Lectures,* by Starrhill Press, an imprint of Elliott & Clark Publishing, Inc., Washington, DC.

All rights reserved, including the right of reproduction in whole or in part in any form. For permission, contact author at Editor@Press53.com, or at the address above.

Cover design by Vicki Latimer Roan

Printed on acid-free paper

ISBN 978-1-935708-04-9

Contents

Introduction   vii

CHAPTER ONE
Why We're Afraid to Perform   1

CHAPTER TWO
Why We Don't Need to Fear Our Audiences   17

CHAPTER THREE
How to Make Your Entrance   33

CHAPTER FOUR
How to Deliver Your Message   47

CHAPTER FIVE
How to Make Your Exit   55

CHAPTER SIX
How to Create a Performing Persona   65

CHAPTER SEVEN
How to Involve Your Audience in Your Performance   79

CHAPTER EIGHT
How to Handle Performance Disasters   93

CHAPTER NINE
How to Become a Star   101

Introduction

> I was in a literal state of shock from the moment I started toward the front of the room until at least ten minutes after it was over. I remember that someone asked a question, but I don't remember what it was, or what I answered, or even *if* I answered. After that question it's all a blank. I know time must have passed, but it's as though I wasn't there. One minute I was standing at the front of the room, and the next minute I was back in my seat. But I couldn't remember how I got there or what else might have happened in between. It was horrible. Just horrible!

The setting for this scene is not a police interrogation room. It's a church parish hall. The speaker is neither a suspect nor a victim in some hideous crime. She's a friend who, in other circumstances, is a sophisticated, competent businesswoman who had been asked to give a short report at her church's annual meeting.

> I can't remember anything I said, just the feeling of being out of control. I think I may have babbled. I think I must have looked and sounded like a monkey chattering in a tree. It was one of the most embarrassing experiences of my life!

Although she gave her report two years ago, the humiliation she felt then is still with her, tightening her voice and twisting her body.

> The worst part of it all is that logically I know there was no reason to fall apart as I did. It was just a report,

just putting what had happened on the record, nothing controversial. The room was familiar, I knew almost everyone there . . . but they became just faces . . . they were all looking at me. *She shudders*. I never, ever want to go through anything like that again!

What my friend has described so well is a fear that is familiar to most of us. We often call this fear stage fright, but it's not, as we might suppose, limited to those who are shy or introverted, nor is it simply a fear of being on stage. This fear is as close as most of us will get—outside of our worst nightmares—to absolute terror. Its symptoms are primal, similar to the innate fight or flight responses that are triggered when we face physical danger: our palms sweat, our hands shake, and our knees tremble. Our pulses race, our breathing rates are short and uneven. Our mouths go dry and our throats tighten; if we don't lose our voices completely, we don't recognize the sounds coming from our mouths. We experience lightheadedness, dizziness, memory loss, even dissociation—our minds seem to separate from our bodies. Our sense of time collapses, as does our sense of self-control. A rush of adrenalin disorients or overwhelms us. Nausea and incontinence threaten.

My friend knew she was not in physical danger when she gave her report. She knew that the members of her church were not going to mob her and gouge out her eyes, but that knowledge didn't help her regain her sense of control. Instead, it magnified her sense of failure.

"How stupid I am," we say to ourselves when we know that we know better. "How humiliating to have lost control when there was no reason to!"

The *Oxford Universal Dictionary* defines stage fright as "extreme nervousness experienced by an actor on the stage, esp. on his first appearance." Performance anxiety, the clinical label for stage fright, expands the definition to include any situation in which we are exhibiting ourselves to or entertaining an audience. Both terms limit our understanding of an anxiety that is so common that we accept its milder manifestations in our everyday, nonstage life as normal.

Introduction

A job applicant's legs begin to shake during an interview; she clutches at them in an attempt at control, then discovers that her sweaty hands have left wet blotches on her new suit and her hands are stained navy blue. Memories of this first post-college interview, and others like it, are now chaining her to a job she outgrew long ago.

A teacher intends to object to a proposal in a faculty meeting, but "freezes up" when comments are requested. She cannot force a sound from her throat. Then, because she hasn't voiced her objections, she feels she must raise her hand along with the other "yea's" when the vote is called, a vote that is contrary to her principles and many years of experience. She drives home feeling like a coward. Little wonder that she "hates" faculty meetings.

A young man hyperventilates before his first date, and his voice, which had settled into the bass range months ago, now threatens to revert to soprano. Although these symptoms have nothing to do with lust, they are so terrifying that they at least momentarily drive lust out of his conscious mind and down into the unconscious where it remains associated with fear.

Each of these persons exhibited one or more symptoms of stage fright or performance anxiety, even though none of them were on stage, none of them were actors, and none of them were performing in the literal sense. Two of the above examples did not occur in front of an audience, which is usually defined as a *group* of people listening to a performer–in fact, the "performer" in the last incident was alone when he experienced the symptoms.

What, then, is the common thread that runs through these experiences?

The intensity of the symptoms may vary, but all of us feel some amount of anxiety whenever we present ourselves to people by whom we expect to be judged. When we are "stage frightened" we are assuming that an uneven distribution of power exists—it's us against them and they've got all the power. When we are "performance anxious" we are anticipating rejection, failure, and consequent humiliation.

For many of us, the anxiety we experience in such situations is so intense that it reaches the level of trauma. It can limit career advancement, as in the case of the interviewee, or determine career choice.

> A young law graduate passes the bar exam but never practices law. His clerkship convinces him that he is inadequate as a public speaker, so he becomes a financial administrator, a career in which "money talks," but he does not.

This anxiety can limit our roles, and therefore our satisfaction, in our social and business communities, as it did for the church member and the teacher. It can even isolate us from society.

> A young woman's fear of social gatherings has led to increasingly severe postparty migraines. By the time she reaches 40, the migraines begin earlier—while she's dressing for a party—and have become so incapacitating that she turns down all invitations not directly related to her profession.

This anxiety can affect our intimate relationships, as it did for the young man anticipating his first date, and can lead to loneliness and bitterness.

> A 50-year-old man, after three failed marriages, has established a career in which he works an 80-hour week

Introduction

alone in his office, and in which his relationships with others are conducted by telephone.

There may be many other factors, both psychological and circumstantial, that lead to our building such barriers in our lives. However, if we agree with Shakespeare that "all the world's a stage," then to the extent that we become effective actors in the world we will all be subject to stage fright in some form. We may not be standing on a raised stage in a theater; our audience may consist of one person; but if we are mentally and emotionally expecting our performance to be judged by that audience and if the audience or the role or the material we're performing is unfamiliar, the terrors of stage fright are as likely to descend upon us as if we were making our first appearance on *The Tonight Show*.

Of course we all want to avoid trauma. If we aren't able to eliminate performance from our lives, our next inclination is to try to eliminate the terror surrounding it. We can't. Anxiety is an appropriate part of any performance; fighting against any appropriate emotion only increases its effects. If we believe that we will only perform well when we are free from anxiety, we will be doomed to failure from the beginning. We'll then carry that failure with us into the next performance, and the next, creating a vicious cycle.

Can we control stage-fright symptoms? Perhaps even use the excitement and adrenalin rush to our advantage?

> The attorney/financial advisor who had been afraid of speaking in public has been responsible for changing the financial basis of his international organization by presenting his plan to member groups across the continent. He says, "I've found my voice."

> A housewife with no prior experience began her own business and operated it so successfully that when she was ready to sell it and move on to a new life-phase she was able to choose from a number of qualified buyers.

She says, "I learned how to get a 'yes' answer from people who intended to say 'no.'"

A percussionist reports on a very bad night. She tripped and fell flat on stage; she split a drumhead with her stick; then the stick got caught inside the drum and she had to struggle to get it out. "I got at least ten compliments on my performance. Everyone thought it was all part of my act."

The confidence that comes from successful performance can enrich our entire lives, freeing us to find new opportunities, to take risks, to speak up, to take charge.

CHAPTER ONE

Why We're Afraid to Perform

I've defined stage fright or performance anxiety as the fear or anxiety experienced when we present ourselves to one or more people by whom we expect to be judged. If we remember telephone calls we had to steel ourselves to make, and letters or memos we avoided writing, we could expand our definition to include the anxiety we feel not only when we present ourselves personally, but even when we present ourselves through media. When we remember how we felt before some (or all) examinations or work assignments, we could even expand the definition of performance to include "the accomplishment, carrying out, doing of any action or work" (The Oxford Universal Dictionary again) that we expect to be judged by others.

In the best of all worlds, this expansion of our definition might ease our fears. Most of us have learned how to reduce anxiety in at least one of our presentation modes, so why don't we apply those lessons to all other modes?

Unfortunately, most of us fervently believe that the performance limits we have set for ourselves are inborn and, therefore, out of our control. We are different, more limited than the fortunate few who are able to talk, sing, and dance in front of hundreds, even thousands of people.

Of course this belief isn't true. I've worked with clients who had been diagnosed with Down syndrome and Alzheimer's disease, with Asperger syndrome and autism. They all learned to perform before an audience. With limitations, of course. An Alzheimer's patient didn't know why she was standing in front of an audience, but she had a marvelous time singing for them.

Each of us has a different array of talents—that is, aptitudes for acquiring certain skills—but every human being has the potential to achieve some level of proficiency in any skill possessed by any other human being.

Performance is a skill, a discipline that can be learned like any other. Six-year-old children can learn to perform in public successfully; so can sixty-year-old retirees.

We are not alone in our fears. Some performance anxiety seems to grip each one of us. Even professional performers who say, "I'm never nervous on stage. It's like the stage is my home," will then go on to list each of their performing terrors.

When we find a human phenomenon that seems to be universal, we assume it must stem from an innate protective device that, at some point in our long evolution, became genetically programmed. But what does performance anxiety protect us from? Neither the individual performer nor the society in which he performs is harmed by the act of performance. In fact, the reverse is true—no culture could survive without its storytellers, its dancers, its musicians, its artists. Culture is developed, maintained, and transmitted through performance.

Performance anxiety does derive from an innate protective device, but one that develops primarily from an internal mechanism that maintains our physiological balance, rather than from an external physical threat.

Strange as it may seem, our anxiety rises from an essential aspect of performance—our interest in what or for whom we are performing. When we believe strongly in protecting the environment, or when we fall in love with a piece of music or a theatrical role, or when we are sure of the unreasonableness of the county tax system, we begin to long for the ability and opportunity to share our beliefs with others–in other words, to perform. If we express our convictions privately to several people, they are likely to suggest that others would want to hear our opinions or our music. Word gets around, and we may be asked to perform.

Or we may have been engrossed in our work on an advertising campaign, or on the five-year forecast for a new wind farm. Now it's time to present our work to colleagues or management.

As soon as we become excited about the performance itself, rather than the material we intend to perform, we find ourselves in the throes of anxiety. We imagine dozens of humiliating outcomes, from hyperventilation to stumbling as we enter the room, and the mental recordings begin playing: "I can't sing," or "I don't sing well enough," "No one wants to hear what I have to say," "I'm stupid," "This idea is too weird (or too familiar)."

In this sequence–interest, excitement, anxiety–lies the clue to the origins of performance anxiety. We are born with internal mechanisms that encourage the development of and are responsible for the protection of our bodies, our minds, and our concepts of self. According to affect theory, a psychological theory developed by Silvan Tomkins, these mechanisms, or affects, are a system of genetically programmed action patterns that respond to certain activators. When we are babies, affects serve not only as internal monitors but, because they are displayed first in our faces, they also serve as external communicators. A sudden noise surprises a baby, the baby's affect system responds, and anyone watching the baby can easily understand that the baby has been surprised by the noise.

In infancy, the affect "shame-humiliation" serves as a balancing mechanism that interrupts a baby's interest in, or enjoyment of some aspect of his surroundings before he becomes overly excited, before his heartbeat or his breathing rate accelerate beyond their normal ranges. (Affect theory labels these mechanisms in terms of a range of response: interest-excitement, for example, and surprise-startle.)

When a baby nears his excitement threshold, the shame affect is triggered: he lowers his eyes, drops and averts his head, blushes, and breaks the interaction.

At two to three months of age, we can observe the same reactions, or even stronger ones, such as crying, when the interaction is broken off by someone else—when a moving object is taken away, or when his mother leaves him. At eight to ten months, the shame reactions can occur if a stranger tries to interact with the baby.

We can think of these mechanisms as the precursors to emotions, which are a blend of the affect and our associations with previous experiences of the affect. Over time, the affect that began as a neurophysiological protective response acquires an emotional biography, and the innate response that preserves our physical and mental balance becomes entangled with memories of losing control of our physical functions, memories of broken relationships, and memories of failures in new situations for which we didn't know the rules. What was originally a universal physiological response has now become an individual psychological response, as well.

As our shame responses become more complex, they often involve the fear-terror and/or the anger-rage responses. For some of us, every failure we've experienced, every humiliation, every negative assessment by others, can congeal into a shame biography that affects our entire sense of self. What was once a simple aversion of the eyes and head is now a disproportionate response to excitement so huge that we may say after a small social gaffe: "I wanted to die," "I wanted the floor to open up and swallow me."

Each new audience, or each new presentation before a familiar audience, is therefore both a source of excitement and a potential source of extreme humiliation. This sounds like a no-win situation. If we're interested enough in a performance to get excited, a sense of shame and humiliation may be triggered. If we're not interested in every aspect of our performance, the audience won't be interested either, and we'll add another humiliating experience to our lengthening list.

Why We're Afraid to Perform

In fact, we need to be more than interested to perform successfully. We need to be excited. If we become too comfortable with the material we are performing or with our audiences, we may feel protected from the possible shame affect, but lose the strength, sensitivity, and mental alertness that a state of excitement can give us—the very state that triggers the shame and anxiety.

Our challenge as performers is not to eliminate anxiety, but to use it. By merely recognizing and accepting the essential function of the shame affect, we take an important step toward successful performance. Performance anxiety is normal. Performance anxiety is necessary to our general well-being.

You'll find, as you work through the exercises in this book, that when you've reduced performance anxiety to a manageable level, you will be able to use any remaining anxiety to improve your performance. You may even find that, on days when you're not feeling up to par, you will need to artificially generate enough excitement to trigger some anxiety.

When we're faced with anxiety situations, most of us have trouble separating our excitement from our fear. They both seem to surface at the same time, and they have similar effects on our breathing and pulse rate.

Let's take a job interview as an example. You hear about a job opening from a friend. Your qualifications seem right; the friend says she'll recommend you for an interview. You research the company through other friends and your library; you review, and perhaps adjust, your resume; you buy a new suit and polish your shoes. During this process, as you and the job seem to be an increasingly perfect fit, your expectations rise. At some point, however, perhaps when you call to set up the interview, the interest-excitement that has prompted you to prepare so diligently can trigger both the shame affect, with its scenarios of past failures, and the fear affect, with its scenes of a future in which you're jobless and homeless.

Our excitement and shame affects can become so intertwined that our response can become habitual. A singer was backstage preparing for another performance. She began to talk about how nervous she was getting, that she was afraid she would forget her words, that her voice wasn't . . . Suddenly she stopped herself, and said, "Wait! This is just excitement! I don't need to go through my nervous routine!"

Keep in mind that there is an excitement threshold that triggers anxiety. That threshold may be different for each of us, so you'll want to identify your own trigger point.

Observe what goes on internally when you prepare for a party, a meeting, or any other event in your daily life that makes you anxious. At what point does excitement change to anxiety? When do the little voices inside your head begin to tell you that you'll be a dud at the party, say the wrong thing at the meeting, that you're not attractive, not smart, a failure? That's your trigger point. That's the level of excitement that you can tolerate before the shame affect kicks in.

Our objective is not to eliminate anxiety entirely, but to get rid of the excess and manage the rest. You can monitor your level of excitement by monitoring your expectations. I'm not suggesting that you live a monotone life with neither expectations nor excitement, only that one way we can reduce anxiety is to look realistically at our expectations.

Review your anxiety triggers of the past few days. Was some of your excitement related to your expectations of the event? Sometimes we fantasize that we will meet our perfect love at a party, or that we will be absolutely brilliant at the staff meeting, so brilliant that our boss will publicly acknowledge us with an immediate promotion and raise.

Fantasies can be useful if they lead us to prepare well for a situation but, if we don't also develop a realistic objective for ourselves, we're likely to add another chapter to our shame biographies.

Think about your next party or meeting. Set one small objective for yourself, such as, "I want to meet one new, interesting person at this party," or "At this meeting I want to make one comment about our target market."

Why We're Afraid to Perform

I often suggest to people preparing for job interviews or auditions that "I need this job" is an anxiety-producing statement, not an objective. "I want this job" is a start in the right direction, but even better is, "From what I know now, I want this job. I'm going to use this interview (or audition) to find out more about it and about the people I'd be working with."

I once argued with a man who wanted to hire me. I told him that I was usually a quick study, but that I had been unable to understand his business adequately. I told him that I was not the person he was looking for. Fortunately, he won the argument, and I spent a productive five years at his company.

Was I nervous during that interview? Of course not! Although I badly needed a job at the time, I wasn't interested in this one; I wasn't excited about the possibility of working there; and I had no positive expectations of the interview. Another important factor in reducing my anxiety was that I made the judgment about my ability to do the job well—I didn't give all that responsibility to the interviewer.

Much of our performance energy is wasted by projecting judgments about ourselves onto those around us. We cannot see ourselves clearly from outside ourselves.

Singers cannot hear themselves as others do; they must rely on musical and physical memories to monitor their performances. (Does your speaking voice on a recording sound anything like your voice?) Dancers cannot see themselves dance because the very act of looking into a mirror changes the dance; they must trust their inner rhythm, muscle memory, and sense of balance. Painters cannot see their paintings during the creative process as others will see it; they are literally, as well as figuratively, too close. They must train an inner eye that can translate a distant bird into one brushstroke that will be retranslated by a viewer into a distant bird.

Our external view of ourselves will always be distorted, so we must develop inner guidelines to monitor our performances. Go back to the party or meeting for which you set one realistic objective.

After you can imagine yourself achieving it, ask yourself the following questions: Who do you expect will be there? Which of them are you casting in the role of your judge? (No fair saying everyone.) Look around the room in your imagination and pick out no more than three of your severest critics. What do you expect they will say or do to let you know that you don't measure up? What will they think? Assess your level of anxiety. Give it a fear number from one to ten.

When, in this process, did you forget your objective?

Focus on your objective again. Now, one at a time, replace your three judges with your three best friends. After each replacement ask yourself what he or she will say, do, or think about you, and reassess your anxiety level.

Could you retain your objective throughout the process? Can you still imagine achieving it?

Remember in as much detail as possible your last performance or the last social or business situation in which you felt overwhelmed by anxiety. Remember every anxious thought you had. Replay the scenario several times, each time changing just one external aspect. Change the setting, the members of the audience, the seating arrangements, the time of day, until you find an acceptable anxiety level.

Did you feel powerless at any time? Did your sense of powerlessness decrease as you gained more control over the situation? At what point did the anxiety level become acceptable to you? Remember, we don't want an anxiety-free performance. You only want to find the level of anxiety you can easily tolerate.

Go back over the scenario again in its original setting, with all the original audience there. Think of one response you wish you'd given at a party, one issue you didn't raise at a meeting, or any other short response in a situation where you're usually anxious but feel you have something important to say. Focus as clearly as you can on the content of the message. Imagine yourself communicating that message to your audience.

Did the change of focus from the judgment of others to the content of your material effect your sense of powerlessness? Your anxiety level?

As you learn to recognize and understand your physical and emotional responses before, during, and after performance, you'll find them far more trustworthy than your imagined audience judgments. You'll also find that you'll use real critiques from your audiences, both positive and negative, as validations of your own responses rather than as judgments.

Communication means, literally, to share with others. We say about an actor who has grown stale in his role, "He was just walking through his part." He was no longer sharing anything with us but his presence. Amateurs can often be distinguished from professional performers because they "say" their lines or "read" their lectures rather than believing in their role or their message and transmitting that belief to us.

My 18-month-old granddaughter gave me a wonderful lesson about the difference between communication and talking. When she wanted to communicate with me, her entire body was intent on trying to tell me what she was observing or thinking, and her voice, as it rose and fell in pitch, sounded as though she were using real English words and phrases. Her speech patterns were so convincingly like my own language that I felt frustrated (and rather stupid) at not being able to understand her language.

But when she talked on her toy telephone, she balanced on one foot, stared out the window, and babbled without inflection—a perfect imitation of her favorite aunt's telephone conversations.

Your audience will try very hard to understand what you are saying if your objective is to communicate a message. But they won't care if you don't care.

If you focus on how perfectly you're delivering your message, so will your audience. You will have turned them into critics.

If you imitate someone else, as my granddaughter did so well, you invite comparisons. Your audience will spend time thinking about who you remind them of, as I did, somewhat guiltily.

Record yourself. Use the short response you wish you'd been able to say, but didn't, from the earlier exercise or any brief, fully sincere statement. First, record yourself doing the worst possible job you can imagine. Focus on what you're saying. Say it with conviction, but make a real mess of how you say it. Next, record the best possible delivery you can imagine. (Rehearse as much as you like, but only record this second attempt once.)

Now listen to both attempts. If the first time you listen to the recording you get caught up in judgments about yourself (such as, "I sound stupid" or "My voice is horrible"), rather than judgments about the performance, replay the recording several times until you can respond to it objectively as an audience member might.

Did your first attempt have some aspects you'd like to keep in a final performance? Some enthusiasm? Did your second attempt sound a bit stiff? Did the quality of your voice change in the second attempt? Did your focus shift to your imaginary judges during the second attempt?

Now record yourself at a level halfway between the worst and the best you can imagine, focusing again on what you want to communicate. Listen to all three. Could you achieve your communication objective with the third attempt?

Humans are sensory beings. We communicate with others from internal sensory images.

When I tell someone about the collision that occurred in front of me today, I speak from my memories of seeing two cars collide, of hearing the screech of brakes, the twisted crunch of metal against metal, the crackling of shattered glass, and my own scream, of feeling my hands tighten on the steering wheel and my foot driving the brake pedal into the floor, of smelling burnt rubber and fear and escaping radiator steam.

Until the memory begins to fade, I will act out the scene with each telling. My foot will unconsciously press against an imaginary brake pedal; my voice will rise in pitch. Even weeks later when I make a general statement about the dangerous intersection of Mill Road and Cathedral Boulevard, I will be abstracting from specific memories of the accident I saw there.

Why We're Afraid to Perform

The more specific we are in our internal image-making, the better we will communicate. Replay the recording you made earlier. Does the delivery of at least one of your statements trigger a related memory? Can you remember what you were thinking as you recorded it?

Record it once more, this time from a mental image that draws on as many senses as possible. For example, if your statement was about your company's target market, see and hear a specific customer in a detailed setting. Listen to all four of your performances. Which was the easiest to perform? Which carries the most conviction?

Humans are storytellers. We try to understand our lives, and the events around us by creating stories. Until we learned to scratch symbols that represented our words, we told our history, our beliefs, our warnings, and our fears in stories, in parables, and myths.

We remember best what we hear or read in story form.

If the last recording you made reminded you of a story about that customer, tell it. What did she say that makes her a representative of your target market? Did she describe her use of your product with a story?

The purpose of performance is communication, not perfection. We have been looking at anxiety during performance up to this point, and we will discuss many other control methods before we are finished. But now let's look at another point in the performance process when anxiety erupts.

In the interview example, when you reviewed your resumé, bought your new suit, and shined your shoes, you were acting from past experience or advice and doing so with a minimum of anxiety. Perhaps you had forgotten to shine your shoes at an interview years ago and have reminded yourself ever since to get those shoes shined early.

A tolerable level of anxiety is necessary and desirable. When we imagine what could go wrong we can prepare remedies and make choices. That's what rehearsals are for. If you worry about what to say if the interviewer asks why you left your last job, you can practice possible answers with a friend. If you worry about losing your voice, you can practice breathing exercises.

Most professional performers have developed elaborate preparatory rituals for themselves—how much sleep they need the night before, how much time they need for checking sound and lighting systems, how much time they need alone in the dressing room, which totems (such as a stuffed animal or pictures) to carry with them.

The rider attached to a professional performer's contract may have pages and pages specifying transportation and hotel arrangements, how the stage is to be prepared, what food is to be available in the dressing room, and how it is to be prepared. The rider in one famous folksinger's contract even specifies in detail the eating utensils that must be provided for her. Each item in the rider has been added because the performer has learned, through trial and error, the conditions that will lead to her best performance.

Make a "worry list" for your next performance. Write your concerns about what could go wrong in one column. As you take a positive, preventive action, enter it in a second column.

If you're worried about not having enough preparation time, make a timeline: working backward from your performance date, schedule each aspect of your preparation.

After the performance, review your actions, changing any that didn't work as well as you'd expected. If one rehearsal wasn't enough, schedule two next time.

Make a checklist of actions for the next performance. Include unplanned actions that helped the performance. If the program started a half-hour late and you used that time to go over the main points of your speech, plan to give yourself an extra half-hour before your next performance.

Expect your checklist to grow longer the more often you perform, just as the professional performer's contract rider grows longer. Although we work toward the best possible performance, perfection doesn't happen often—perhaps twice in a lifetime of professional performance—and never when we expect it.

If we believe we must give a perfect performance, we will be flooded with an overload of anxiety. How many perfect games does a pitcher need to get into the Baseball Hall of Fame?

Most of us could recite the "two times x" multiplication table perfectly, but not many audiences would be willing to walk across the street to watch us do that. It is the very risk of live performances, the fact that anything can happen, that attracts audiences.

Our educational system was developed to produce workers in industry, where widgets have to fit perfectly onto gizmos. We have been trained to believe that only a perfect test score is acceptable, and we often go through life trying to get an A from everyone—our boss, our spouse, our friends, our children, even strangers we meet at a party.

But when we enter the work force, if we're not working on a factory production line, we have the opportunity to learn about being good enough to get the job done. No advertising campaign proposal is perfect in every detail; it just needs to be good enough to win the assignment. No corporate merger is perfect; at best, it's a compromise with which all parties can live. No law is perfect; one person's protection under the law often leads to another's loss of freedom.

Performance is a creative activity. When we perform, we are creating something that has never happened before in exactly the same way. Even if we have given the same speech many times, the audience will be different each time. Because each performance is new, there is no way to foresee every detail that could affect it negatively.

During any creative process we are likely to encounter a different type of anxiety that may be a normal, perhaps even a necessary aspect of creativity.

Partway into the process, usually after we've made some progress toward our goal, we hit a spot where nothing goes right. We reread what we've written and find it horrible, or we have a rehearsal or practice session filled with disasters, and we go into a funk: "What I've written is trash," "I can't sing," "Why did I ever think I could act/practice law/market this product?" If we have the pressure of a deadline to meet, we add several despairing, panic-filled thoughts: "I'll quit my job tomorrow," "I'll run away," or worse.

Painful as it is, this type of anxiety-ridden depression is often the turning point in the creative process. I believe that the courage to work through this type of anxiety is the defining characteristic of the successful creator.

Anxiety is a natural part of the creative process because we are creating something new, something that's never been said or written or interpreted quite this way before. If we are truly creating something that is new, something that we've not previously known, experienced, invented, or understood, we literally won't know what we're creating until we've created it.

We had to start from an old or known perspective; there's no other possible starting place. The reason you hate what you've written or how you interpreted that song is that during your work on the project you lost your old, familiar perspective and are now in new, uncharted territory. You've crossed the boundary from old to new, and in doing so you've changed, and the original goal must now be changed. Anxiety floods in when you recognize at some level of consciousness that what you are doing is completely different from what you had thought you were doing.

When I began to write one of my short stories, I intended to write about love. At some point, three men wandered into the story, one after the other, and I became terribly frustrated because I couldn't make them behave as I had intended lovers should behave. I couldn't seem to get rid of them, either; whenever I began a new draft one or another of these men would appear.

One summer night, after what must have been my sixteenth wrestling session with the story, I ended up on the living room couch in utter despair. "It's not the story, it's you. You can't write. Why did you think you were a writer? If you can't write, why are you living?" I stared at the open front door and gave myself the final, sad proof that I was the most inept person ever to try to write: "See? You could never, ever in a million years convey on paper the play of streetlight and shadow on that door. What made you think you could write about love?"

The next night I had to force myself to sit at the typewriter. Grumbling, making noises of disgust, I reread all the drafts. Gradually I realized that I had not been writing the definitive story about love after all. I had been writing a story about three men who were running away from what they loved.

After I knew what I was writing about, finishing the story was relatively easy.

I can now recognize this creative form of anxiety for what it is. I call it my couch-and-door depression. It can still be painful and awful at times, but I do know that tomorrow, or some day soon, if I keep at my project, I will discover what it is that I'm doing.

This form of anxiety is often intermingled with anger—anger at oneself, at a boss, at a teacher, at a boyfriend—and seems to occur just before a major breakthrough in a project, or in an entire career.

When we begin to deal with performance anxiety realistically, we find we are dealing with an anxiety calendar. We can't program each anxiety period to arrive at specific moments in our lives when we are prepared to handle them beautifully, but it's helpful to know that they follow a pattern.

The first round of anxiety may come as soon as a performance is scheduled. "Aargh! What do you mean, the first sales presentation for the new product is tomorrow? I'm not ready!" Hopefully, we worry enough about our performance to prepare for the presentation as well as we can, making our best judgments about the questions that may be raised, putting together our charts or projections, rehearsing what we will say in front of as many colleagues as we can find.

Partway through the development of our presentation we may be assaulted by a deeper anxiety that makes its appearance as depression. "The sales pitch is all wrong for this customer, the product is a joke, and I'm a rotten salesman." If we don't give up, but use this round of anxiety to help us reassess the presentation, we may reach a fairly high level of confidence in our material and how we will present it.

Then, boom! Sometime between the sound of the alarm clock next morning and the first words at the presentation, the third round of performance anxiety will hit. "I can't stand up in front of those people." This is the round that we call stage fright because–horror of horrors!–we will have an audience.

The focal points of our bouts of performance anxiety often shift in a sequence similar to this example: from material, to self, to audience.

CHAPTER TWO

Why We Don't Need to Fear Our Audiences

A brilliant young multimedia artist described a common experience when we analyzed her last piece of performance art: "I thought I was protecting myself from the audience, but instead I was putting my fear between us."

Our greatest anxieties about performing are audience focused: "They'll laugh at me," "They'll hate me," "They'll walk out." The variations we can play on this theme are endless. A favorite modification runs along these lines: "I'll forget what I wanted to say," "I'll make a fool of myself," "I'm not good enough to . . ." In this variation, the audience reaction is only implied, but the underlying assumption we make is still the same—the audience has nearly unlimited power and the performer has none.

Most audiences give, or want to give, a great deal of power to the performer and are disappointed when that power is not exercised. If they didn't expect to receive something of at least equal value, why would someone be willing to pay $1200 to see Barbra Streisand perform? Or travel two hundred miles for a poetry reading? Or give up three hours out of a busy day to attend a software demonstration?

Why have so many of us turned the power formula of performance backward and against ourselves?

Many potential performers equate performance with powerlessness (and with the terror that results from being powerless) because they literally had little or no power at their first performance. A young woman told me a story that contains elements common to many first performances:

> I learned my part perfectly for the first-grade play. I was in my daisy costume, very excited to be performing. I watched as the auditorium filled with everyone else's parents and grandparents and brothers and sisters. Suddenly I realized my parents weren't coming, and they were the only ones who weren't. I began to cry and I couldn't stop. I ran to a corner, sobbing, and nothing the teacher said could make me go on stage.

Today, as an adult, "Daisy" remembers the incident as one of the most humiliating experiences of her life, an experience that was somehow her fault, and an experience that proved to her that she was inherently unable to perform. She would love to perform the songs she writes, but instead she gives them away to "real" performers.

Various elements of that first performance did deprive Daisy of power as a child, but they no longer apply in her adult life.

When we are young, literally small, we do not have the power to control our environments. Adults, the big people in our lives, have power over us, and we learn to equate power with size. Even if Daisy had become reasonably comfortable rehearsing her role in front of her class, at the actual performance the audience size tripled before her eyes and so did the size of individuals in the audience. In child terms, each adult who entered the auditorium diminished her power and control.

The equation, size = power, or bigger = better, pervades much of our thinking. When the first Japanese-made miniature radio arrived at what was then RCA Laboratories, all the engineers who listened to it before it was tested pronounced its sound quality inferior to standard-size radios. Only after sound tests proved its quality to be superior to the then-standard radio did the engineers acknowledge that their judgment had been biased because of the radio's small size.

If Daisy's teacher had been wiser, she would have prepared her young performers by asking them to imagine lots of grown-ups watching them. She could have discussed with them how they might feel in front of all those big people. She might have invited an increasing number of adults to observe final rehearsals.

If Daisy's parents had been wiser, they would have asked some other adult to give Daisy support (in her terms, protection). Few of us outgrow the need for such support. That's why a sports team is said to have an advantage when they play at home. Many professional performers use fans, groupies, even paid claques for support. They use managers, agents, and other employees for protection. Stage performers, musicians, and athletes all have unions to support and protect them. Contracts protect professional performers; even the size of their fees can give them a sense of protection.

The second power element in Daisy's first experience with an audience was lack of choice. Presenting a play wasn't her idea, it was the teacher's. Nor was Daisy able to decide whether or not to invite a large audience, which play she was to perform in, or even the role she was to play. All these decisions were made by a powerful adult.

Few of these conditions hold for adults, who are able to make many more choices about their lives than Daisy could as a child. Some of us are more comfortable selling by phone than door-to-door; for others, the reverse is true. Some of us are more comfortable performing on a playing field than on a stage. Some stage performers feel confined by a playwright's words and prefer to write their own material. In Daisy's case, her dream is to sing her own songs, not give them to someone else, but she has never seen the disparity between her own talents and desires and her first-grade failure.

A third power element in Daisy's first performance was the teacher's role as judge; that's the role our educational system gives to teachers.

Performance anxiety is the anxiety you experience when you present yourself to one or more people by whom you expect to be judged. For most of us, our first teachers are our first judges outside our families—our original judges and first audiences.

Even if we aren't given a letter grade for our childhood performances, a comment about our performing abilities is likely to appear on the report card. Our teachers, however, are seldom trained in performance, and their uninformed judging can seriously damage young performers.

A successful businesswoman in her early 50s asked if I would help her prepare for an entry into politics. An appropriate goal, I thought. She was poised, always tastefully dressed, and had climbed the ladder to corporate management from the very bottom.

We began each session with some singing exercises to strengthen her voice, then worked on a simple speech about her political beliefs. She forgot to bring her speech to the fourth session, so we used a book from my library and worked on how to use humor in a speech. When she came to the next session, she had forgotten to bring both her speech and my book. I pointed out how much progress she had made in the singing exercises, and she began to cry:

> Sister Mary Catherine told me I couldn't sing. She said I was spoiling all the songs. She said I had to stand in the back row at the Christmas concert and just move my mouth, but not let a sound out. And I was short, and everyone else in the back row was tall, so everyone at the concert knew why I was in the back row.

How sad that, for a month and a half, such a competent woman had been afraid to tell me what her real goal was and that, for more than forty years, she had denied herself the pleasure of singing.

She is not unique in having blocked out old, old fantasies of who she wanted to be and what she wanted to do. Both men and women have cried in my studio when they realized they no longer had to deny their fantasies.

Why We Don't Need to Fear Our Audiences

Sometimes family members, as well as educators, feel they are protecting children from future disappointment if they tell them they don't have the ability to sing, play football, or paint a picture.

Seldom do professional performers in any field make such disparaging remarks to children. They know personally that the most important attribute for any performer is the desire to perform. If they recognize that desire in a child, they encourage it.

We can change the power equation. As adults, we can recondition ourselves. We can, first of all, recognize the reality of the *size* = *power* element in our childhood experiences, and reassess our power in nonperforming adult situations.

Go back over your last good day, a day in which everything seemed to go well. In which events did you have some control over the outcome? This is a hard exercise. Most of us are conditioned to give all the credit to others or to external forces. So if you baked and decorated a beautiful cake or built a handsome desk, don't be satisfied with saying, "It was a good recipe," or "I had a beautiful piece of wood to work with." At least add, "I followed the recipe exactly," or "I used the woodgrain to good advantage."

Control, even minimal control, is power. We often think of control as being either absolute, as in, "I've got everything under control," or non-existent, as in, "That child is completely out of control." Those who believe that they are in absolute control of a situation are so often tense in body and voice that I suspect they are carrying over their potty-training—when they learned to "control" with a sphincteric contraction—to tight-fisted relationships in their adult lives.

We often think of power in terms of relationships—who has power over whom.

Personal power exists whenever we are free to make choices. If we redefine control as the freedom and ability to make choices, we are taking the first step away from a sense of powerlessness.

Practice performance power by staging a performance in your

living room. Invite one supportive person as an audience. Plan what you will wear, where your friend will sit, where you will stand, which lamps will be lit. Choose your performance material carefully—read a paragraph or two from a book you love, or prepare a short speech about something you care about. Rehearse it. This exercise is not for the purpose of performing perfectly, but of gaining a sense of control over the circumstances surrounding our adult performance and beginning the process of exorcising the memories of performances in which we had little or no control.

Ask your friend to help you in a second exercise. Walk into the room in the most powerless condition you can imagine—use your early childhood memories, if you want. Then re-enter in the most powerful condition you can imagine. Remember that control is power; before you enter, rehearse mentally all the elements of this performance that you have controlled. Or imitate some powerful person as you walk in. Then re-enter in your ordinary power condition, the way you walk on a good day. Ask your friend for feedback on these three entrances.

When potential performers use this exercise, they often find that they think of themselves in the first powerless condition and think of others in the second ideal condition. In reality, they ordinarily walk with a sense of power midway between the two that is comfortable for both themselves and their audiences.

One important element missing from Daisy's first performance, because she never got as far as the stage, is the first experience of a group audience response.

Do you remember the first time you had to stand in front of your class to give a book report? At first all those faces were unrecognizable. "A sea of faces" is a good analogy because in your natural anxiety they seemed to swim and float. Then out of this ocean the playground bullies' faces stood out. Maybe they were paying no attention to you, rolling their eyes toward heaven, or crossing their eyes. Even if they weren't actively being negative toward you or what you were saying, you thought they were. You forgot what you wanted to say, maybe even stuttered. Time seemed endless. Your prayers for the class bell to ring went unanswered.

The best you could hope for was to get the whole thing over with and stumble back to the semi-oblivion of your own seat.

If this scenario is familiar you've probably realized that the power elements we've already described are present here: you were suddenly confronted with the size of the class; you were assigned a performance topic that had little relevance to your interests or talents; you were being judged by a powerful adult. In reality, what was being judged was how well you achieved the teacher's objectives, but it's difficult for a young child to distinguish between self and achievement.

That first audience was required to be present at school. That first audience had little, if any, interest in the content of your book report. You may have assigned a great deal of power to that first audience, but its response was due to the lack of choice (or personal power) felt by each child in the classroom.

The majority of adult audiences attend performances voluntarily. How many books did you read during your school years because someone reported on the book in class? Even adults are not very interested in oral book reports; they'd rather hear the author interviewed.

Individual audience members pursue both conscious and subconscious objectives. The conscious objectives might be to be entertained or to learn about the new recycling initiative or to support a political candidate. Their subconscious objective is to be a part of a crowd, to lose for a period of time their sense of isolation, to laugh or applaud or cheer, even to dissent together with others.

The human desire to become part of a homogeneous crowd is so strong that when an audience is *not* homogeneous our cultural mores will split the space allotted to each group. The courtroom has specific seating arrangements for the jury, the judge, the plaintiff and her legal team, the defendant and her legal team, the witness. Each space is presumed to designate a specific attitude toward the proceedings. The audience for sporting events is split, the home team boosters on one side, visitors on the other. If you've ever sat on the wrong side at a football stadium, you'll remember how strange, isolated, subdued you felt. Our legislatures are seated according to political party. Wedding audiences are also split, the bride's on one side of the aisle and the groom's on the other.

The empowerment of an audience is the result of the performance, not a precondition. When an audience forms voluntarily for any purpose, the individuals in the crowd give up some part of their individuality to the crowd. In a crowd, we want to take our actions together with others. We feel embarrassed if we applaud or laugh at the wrong time—that is, when most of the crowd is not applauding or laughing. The tendency to be a part of the group is so strong that an entire audience can be annoyed by crackling candy wrappers, embarrassed by a drunken heckler, or become angry enough to complain to an authority if a smaller second group threatens to destroy the harmonious response of the majority. If we are in the minority, we may find the majority response intimidating and choose to leave.

We want to respond together as an audience. We find self-affirmation and release when we applaud together at the end of a play. The catharsis that has been the intent of classical theater for 2,000 years is not exclusive to theater. That release is the desire of every audience and is, in itself, empowering.

In effect, the audience gives the performer the responsibility for empowering it.

An audience needs a leader. Because the individuals in an audience have each given up some of their personal power to join a group, they are individually vulnerable. They want and need someone to take care of them. If the performer doesn't accept the responsibility of leadership, audience members will either leave, physically or mentally, or they will make one of their members the leader.

The voluntary audience (remember, that's the most common type of audience) is a responding entity. That is, its members are not there to conduct the orchestra, to lecture, or to carry the football. They are there to respond to the performance.

Why We Don't Need to Fear Our Audiences

It is the performer, then, who is the initiating entity, the one who takes the action, or does the talking. It is the performer who has the responsibility for the audience's response. A voluntary audience gives that power willingly to the performer. That's why they're sitting in the audience and not on the stage or playing field. That's why they need to trust that the performers are more powerful than the audience.

Because an audience gives the performer power, it has a vested interest in the performer's success. A friend and I purchased tickets for a series of dance programs. We arrived at the theatre for the last program without realizing that a mistake had been made when the tickets were issued. We weren't going to see dance that afternoon, but comic performance artists, a program that appealed to neither of us.

But we were already committed to enjoying ourselves. Like other audiences, we had made plans for an enjoyable afternoon together; we had dressed, driven into the city, found a parking place, all of the anticipatory details that build audience commitment. So we stayed, trying very hard to have a good time. As each new comic took the stage, we said, "This one will be better than the last one." We didn't give up hope until the intermission, when we decided to leave.

Even though we were only marginally voluntary audience members because we were not interested in the material being performed, we tried for over an hour to like what was being presented to us. Consider, then, how hard a truly voluntary audience will work for you.

Treat the audience as the entity it has become. In general, each member of the audience is looking for unity and, therefore, equality with other audience members. The very best performances not only help create and maintain a sense of equality among audience members, but also leave them with a sense of equality with the performers by engaging them in the performance process (another way that performers empower audiences). If you imagine yourself making the winning basket as you leave the game, you've been watching a good performer.

A university professor engaged me to critique his lectures. Early in the class, a student asked a question. The professor, pleased by this display of interest, bounded up the steps in the lecture hall to engage the questioner in a lengthy discussion. The other students relaxed; some smirked. The lecture was over as far as everyone else was concerned.

Ten minutes into his next lecture, a hand was raised, a question was asked, and the expectant smirks began. But the professor, now armed with an understanding of performance theory, remained at the podium and included the entire class in his answer. The students' startled reactions clearly indicated that their game was over.

If the performance format asks for or permits questions and comments from the audience, the audience member who makes a comment becomes an individual, separating briefly from the audience. A practiced audience commenter/questioner knows that he has become a performer, a part of the show, and speaks for the audience, including them in his comment. He does not, however, have the same rights and responsibilities as a second performer in a theatrical production has.

When an audience commenter assumes a performer's role, a practiced on-stage performer acknowledges that she has been joined by another performer, but does not relinquish control of the stage (the position of power). On behalf of the audience, she has the right to rephrase questions or comments, to limit their length and their number. All her responses are directed to the audience as a whole.

There are only two types of voluntary audience members that will not work on your behalf—hecklers and adversaries. If you intend to work as a stand-up comic, you will undoubtedly encounter hecklers. Include the audience if you reply.

Alan King gave a great response to an interviewer who asked how he dealt with hecklers. He said that only kids get caught up with them; as a comedian matures he understands that, no matter how clever his reply, he will lose the rest of the audience if he focuses on the heckler.

Why We Don't Need to Fear Our Audiences

If you want to enter local politics, intend to speak on a controversial subject such as abortion, or plan to become a trial attorney, you will encounter adversarial questioners. Their intent is to wrest the stage and its powerful rights from the performer. They want to *become* the performer, without assuming that role's responsibilities.

Even in these special cases, one heckler in an audience of fifty is only one-fiftieth of that audience. Remember that the audience as a whole has a vested interest in *your* performance.

Include the entire audience in your eye and body focus. We are sometimes more self-conscious about performing in front of people we know. If your family, your best friend, the love of your life, or your boss is present in the audience, they will want to merge into the group. Let them.

Direct eye contact between people who are not intimates can be perceived as threatening. Novice Manhattanites are warned never to make eye contact with other subway riders. People who have assaulted strangers describe a sense of terror "because he looked at me," or the disrespect they felt "because he looked at me."

Public-speaking students are often taught that they should make eye contact with each member of the audience, moving from one to another. But that only works when the speaker has the entire audience in her focus. Otherwise, when a performer makes direct eye contact with one audience member, that person feels uncomfortable and everyone else feels excluded.

In some adversarial situations, you may *want* to look directly into an individual's eyes. An attorney, for example, may want to do so when dealing with an unwilling witness, or a teacher with an unruly child. Even in a specific situation where you consciously intend to intimidate by focusing your eyes directly on one person, you will want to include the entire audience in the process of intimidation through your body focus.

We don't often think of our bodies as being composed of many sensory systems that can be consciously focused, even though our language has many references to the body's response to people or situations. Remember that you thought your fourth-grade teacher had eyes in the back of her head? And we say: "The hair stood up on my arms," "She made my skin crawl," "He made me blush," "My blood ran cold," "My heart stopped when I heard his voice," "That was like a kick in the gut."

Our sensory systems gather information. The scientific name for focusing our hearing on one voice or sound out of many is, believe it or not, "cocktail party syndrome." The inability to selectively focus on one sound or voice is considered a hearing dysfunction.

We can also be selective with our eyes or our visual focus. We can focus our eyes on one individual in a group, or on the entire group.

Look out a window or through a doorway into another room. Focus on the farthest tree or object you can see. Notice that all the objects between you and your focal point have become part of your peripheral vision.

Look at some object near you, then look out the window or into the next room again. This time, let your eyes see the entire scene. Your depth perception will not be as acute, but your focus will be wide enough to see everything framed by the window or doorway.

Other audience members will sense that they have become peripheral if you focus all your sensory attention on only one person. Ordinarily, if you focus your mental or emotional attention on one individual in a group, your other sensory organs will also be attentive to him. Your head tends to turn toward that person, your shoulders tend to contract slightly, and your entire body may lean toward him. These physical adjustments give all your sensory systems the best vantage point for picking up information.

But if you then want to learn how the group is responding to that person, your eye focus expands to include the entire group, your body expands, and you may lean back slightly.

Practice body focus the same way you practiced visual focus. Think of your entire body as a system for gathering information. Focus it toward the most distant object. Did you feel drawn to that one object?

Why We Don't Need to Fear Our Audiences

What was your attitude toward the objects between you and the focal point? Refocus on an object near you, then on the scene outdoors or in the next room. Observe what happens to your body. Did you feel an expansion through the chest or shoulders? A relaxation?

When your teacher seemed to have eyes in the back of her head, she was consciously allowing her body to be sensitive to the movement and sound in the room while she was working at the blackboard.

As a performer, allow your body to be aware of everyone in the room, even those behind you, at all times. Then when you need to focus visually on just one individual, you can stay in touch with, and include, the rest of your audience through your expanded body focus.

Maintaining the entire audience in focus is not only necessary for their comfort, but also for the performer's. Any idiosyncratic action by an audience member—falling asleep, coughing, tweeting—can be distracting to a performer unless he is treating the entire group as an entity.

There is only one audience per performance. When an adversarial group rather than a single adversary is present at a performance all of the above audience characteristics still apply.

The town council has invited the public to a hearing on whether to build a new town hall. Even though their objectives for attending the meeting differ, those who oppose building the town hall and those who want to have it built will have come to the hearing voluntarily.

Both groups are interested (sometimes with a vengeance).

Each group will try to sit together for a sense of unity, and they will respond together.

It's tempting for a performer in such a situation to treat the audience as though it were two groups—your side and the other side—and to focus on one or the other. But you will anger the other side if you exclude them from your focus, and if you focus on them exclusively your side will accuse you of pandering to the opposition.

The Eagles' quarterback, after all, is performing for the Redskins' fans, as well as his own, and for all those Monday-morning quarterbacks in front of their TV sets.

All of our premises have been based on the desires, needs, and behavior of a voluntary audience. But the audiences at some business meetings are involuntary, and teachers face these audiences every day. Because the audience (or some large part of it) doesn't want to be present, none of the voluntary audience characteristics apply.

The performer's only solution is to try to engage the interest of the majority of the audience. At that point, the remaining voluntary audience characteristics become active for that majority.

In a classroom, that may mean that not every student will be interested in every class, but you will have an opportunity to engage them, if not by work outside the classroom, then by changing your point of interest for the next class session.

Involuntary business audiences can sometimes be improved by asking uninterested colleagues to assist you. One of them can handle the visuals, another can be asked to begin the discussion.

If you can turn the majority of an involuntary audience into a voluntary audience, they will begin to exert their influence over the uninterested minority. Your own interest in and passion for your subject are powerful conversion tools. In any case, you will want to include the entire audience in your focus at all times.

Understanding your audience and its interests is obviously very important when you're preparing for any performance and essential when preparing for an indifferent or an involuntary audience. Who will form your audience? How old are they? Why will they be there?

You would use different illustrations, perhaps even different language, if you were giving a speech before an audience of schoolchildren or an audience at a retirement village. You would make different sales presentations of software to a hospital and a nonprofit clinic and different presentations to the floor nurses who would use the software and to the hospital board that would buy the software. When you are doing your research, talk to at least one representative member of the audience. Learn as much as you can about what they want.

Individual responses after a performance can help you to prepare for the next performance.

Why We Don't Need to Fear Our Audiences

Don't shy away from negative comments. A performer who was beginning her professional career as a blues singer was devastated when an audience member told her she was singing the wrong material. What he actually said was, "You ought to stick to religious music, honey!" We discovered that if she developed a different on-stage persona, her material was fine. She wouldn't have picked up on that idea as quickly if she hadn't examined that rude comment for some possible usefulness.

I'm not suggesting that you take all audience comments, either positive or negative, at face value.

From an audience's perspective, a performance is a mystical and magical event. Consequently, they don't know quite what to say afterward. How do you describe magic and mystery? The blues singer was wise enough to know that if she loved the blues, she had a right to sing them. Her task, then, was to ferret out the reasons behind the comment.

Other performers are another source of audience information. When your best anecdote seems to fall flat, remembering another performer's comment—"Don't expect much response from that crowd, even if they agree with you"—can be helpful.

The people who make arrangements for the performance are another good source of direct information. They know what went over big last time and what didn't work.

Your objective in audience research is not to change the content of your speech, but rather to plan the best possible presentation of that content.

You may find that some audiences are not for you. If you're a political candidate who has a choice between an audience of the local football boosters club and an audience of local doctors, and you've never seen a football game in your life but are an ardent advocate of revising the healthcare reform bill, you'll want to choose the doctor audience rather than try to find football anecdotes for the other crowd.

Keep in mind during your research that all the individual responses you gather will be replaced by a group response during your performance. You're performing for an audience, not individual audience members. That audience wants to help you give them a good performance.

CHAPTER THREE

How to Make Your Entrance

Any audience, voluntary or involuntary, makes assumptions about the role of a performer and assigns specific responsibilities to the performer. How do we learn to fulfill that role and carry out those responsibilities?

The technique for communication with an audience is different from the technique for one-to-one communication. We quite naturally shift our vocal pitch, the tempo and rhythm of our speech, the content of what we say, and the way we say it when we're speaking to different individuals. We also adapt our bodies to others, changing speed and size of gestures, changing our posture and our walk.

When you speak to a small child, you may use a slightly higher voice pitch, simpler words. You may bend down to talk to him. If the two of you are walking to a playground, you shorten your steps to accommodate his. In other words, you tune your voice and body to the child's age and size.

We also adapt to different personal energy levels. If a friend is excited about a promotion, you will usually raise your own energy level to congratulate her appropriately. If she has just lost a promotion, you may reduce your energy level in order to synchronize it with hers, or you may gradually raise your level in order to cheer her up. Again, you are tuning your energy level to hers.

Much of the information we exchange with each other is conveyed by means other than words. We transmit meaning through vocal tone, pitch, volume, and rhythm, through gesture and posture, through our use of personal energy, through the clothes we wear.

Imagine that you have in front of you three people: a person you despise, your favorite aunt or uncle, and a baby. Say out loud, "I love you," to each person in turn, and notice how the words sounded, which muscles might have tensed or relaxed, which emotions surfaced. You were using the same three words, but with three very different meanings.

Now eliminate the person you don't like and include both of the remaining persons as you say, "I love you." Can you feel and hear the changes in body and voice and emotional level when you are making that statement to two people, rather than just one individual?

You changed the meaning of the three words because the love you felt for the baby is somewhat different from the love you felt for your uncle. Without giving it much thought, you probably came up with an internal meaning of love that was appropriate for that specific combination of people.

That is exactly what should happen when you treat the audience as a group. If you rehearse your performance before just one friend, imagine that a group is present, a group the size of your expected audience.

The larger the audience, the larger you must be. Choose just one imaginary person. Say, "I love you," aloud. Add one more person, then another, then another, each time saying, "I love you," just once to each group.

Notice what happened to your eye focus. Did you look at only one person when you said the phrase? If so, did the emotional content of the phrase shift from a meaning appropriate for the group to a meaning specific to that one person?

Repeat the exercise. As you add each person, enlarge your focus to include the entire group. If the word love has lost its meaning through so much repetition, try "I hate you." (In this case, you may want to change your imaginary people.)

Notice how your body seems to expand as the group grows larger. The expansion of the shoulders may be most noticeable, but perhaps your hand gesture broadened, your rib cage opened, and your stance changed. If the shift was so gradual that you felt no changes, repeat the exercise one more time, but begin with one person and then add four more all at once.

If this imaginary game doesn't work for you, observe your eye and body focus the next time you're talking casually with a few people at lunch or at a party, and someone else joins the group. Or notice what happens to others in the group. The circle widens, eye and body focuses expand to include the new person.

Notice what happens when someone the group doesn't like or doesn't want to join them pulls up a chair. You may see eye and body focuses contract to exclude the outsider; you may hear voices lose enthusiasm; the content of the conversation may change.

A great deal of information, both internal and external, is available to you in your everyday life to help you prepare to be as large as your audience.

Your performance begins before you enter the performing space. The performer's entrance gives the audience its first taste of the performance to come. An entrance is itself an event, a prelude to the performance. An audience very often responds to an entrance with applause; a rock audience yells and whistles; a theatrical audience may interrupt a play to applaud the entrance of a star.

That star actor will already be in character before he appears on stage. He will walk at a tempo appropriate to his character; he will come from an imaginary place offstage with a specific purpose for entering. If he receives applause at his entrance, he will remain in character. The action on stage may freeze until the applause ends, or the actor may add some movement or lines in keeping with his character, or the action may continue through the applause, even though some dialogue may be lost, but modern theatrical conventions do not allow the actor to step out of his character to acknowledge the applause.

When you expand your body focus to include your entire audience, you have begun the process of changing from your ordinary social or professional role to that of performer, just as the actor changed from his everyday role into that of his character.

But the non-actor's entrance has a different purpose and, therefore, a different set of conventions.

From the audience's perspective, the first entrance at any nontheatrical performance acts as the transition between their previous activity as individuals and their present activity as a group. If you are the master-of-ceremonies and the first to speak at an awards dinner, that transition is your responsibility. If you are the first speaker introduced by the master-of-ceremonies, your responsibility is to maintain the audience's "groupness."

We've all attended functions at which equipment or travel problems have delayed the start of the performance. Remember how uncomfortable you felt? How irritated? And how long it took for the performer to change your attitude?

The audience had gathered itself in expectation of a group experience. Without a performer on whom they could rely as a group, any groupness they had achieved splintered into a collection of frustrated individuals.

The larger the audience, the slower its response. When you walk into a conference room where ten other people are gathered, your pace will be slightly slower than your ordinary speed. But imagine walking onto a stage before 10,000 people. All of them must be gathered to attention.

At the beginning of his career, my favorite conductor made his entrances in the mood of the first piece the orchestra was to perform. He was already hearing the music before he came on stage and subconsciously assumed we were as ready as he to participate in it. A single person or a small class of students could have tracked him as he rushed to the podium, but a larger audience needed more time to assimilate his arrival before they were ready for the music to begin. They needed to make the transition from individuals to audience first; then they would have been ready for him to carry them into the music.

When he began to study his entrances, he learned to accommodate his audience's needs while still transmitting his excitement for the music.

On the other hand, the audience energy level at a basketball game requires that the team run, or at least jog, onto the court.

A headliner comic may run onto the stage if his opening act has raised the audience's energy to a very high level, but the size of his audience will determine the pace of his delivery. The laughter of an audience of ten takes less time than the laughter of an audience of a hundred.

The intent of every performer is to move his audience to laughter or other emotional catharsis, or to action. The larger the audience, the more time required to move them. If you tune yourself to the size of the audience and its energy level, you'll find yourself walking and speaking at the correct tempo.

Your entrance establishes or maintains the emotional response of the audience. When you have expanded your body focus to include everyone in the audience, assess its mood and energy level. Is the mood celebratory? Tired? Adapt your own mood to either capitalize on the audience's energy, or to bring them into your mood.

Imagine this scenario: You call an old friend to tell him you've just broken your engagement. Before you get past "How are you?" he tells you he's going to be married. Even though you placed the call, he has become the initiator, not only of information, but of mood and energy level. You have become the responder, and will probably adapt yourself to his mood before you change roles and ask for his comfort. You and your friend may exchange the initiator and responder roles many times before you say good-bye; the emotional character and energy level of the interaction may also change many times.

One of the differences between performance and one-to-one communication is that performance is primarily a one-way conversation. You have the responsibility to initiate all activity; the audience expects to respond. You can use their responses, of course, but you are expected to be in control of the emotional content and energy level of the performance.

Whether you are entering from a hallway or backstage, or seated at a speaker's table, or are already on stage before a curtain goes up, you will want to begin your performance before the audience first sees you.

Enter as a performer. The easiest entrance is from backstage. Whether you're entering from a locker room or literally entering from stage wings, an entrance is easier if you have preparation space out of the audience's view.

Be alone. If you cannot separate yourself physically from business colleagues or backstage personnel, separate yourself mentally. Now is not the time to get involved in someone else's marital or financial troubles, or to discuss how bad the weather is.

Professional performers develop elaborate pre-entrance rituals that can include everything from whether they bathe or shower, how long they stay in the bathtub, when they eat, what they eat, which totems they carry, how early they arrive at the performance space. These rituals may cover the entire 24-hour period before a performance and may be practiced with a superstitious fervor, but they are always based on past experience (what worked the last time) and always idiosyncratic (what works for them).

Take the time to integrate yourself by getting in touch with as much of your body as possible. Feel your feet on the ground, feel yourself breathe. If your shoulder muscles are tense, shake your arms.

Let yourself feel the anxiety. The lump in your throat and the tightness in your chest are real, an innate physical reaction to stress that in earlier times enabled our ancestors to swing from branch to branch through the jungle and throw spears at saber-toothed tigers with all their strength.

Although a performing situation is stressful, we need to override the physical response that prepares us for hand-to-hand combat. Let the anxiety flow down through your entire body. You will find your mind clearer and your arms more free.

A professional back-up singer made her debut as lead singer with a band, performing material she had written. Her audience included many professional musicians, among them her ex-husband—a super-stress situation. She reported how she handled it:

> When I told you before I went on that I was scared, you said, "Of course!" That was just the perfect thing to say. I thought, "Oh, right! There's nothing wrong with being scared. I can use it if I don't fight it." I had my best performance ever. And the best part of all was that I didn't trash myself afterwards about how badly I'd sung, like I used to.

If one of your objectives for a performance is to *eliminate* all anxiety, you are almost certain to fail and, having failed to achieve that objective, you are likely to believe that the entire performance was a failure. You will become involved in overcoming anxiety rather than in the material you're performing and how you're communicating that material to your audience. No matter how well you sing or speak or teach, the constant presence of the anxiety you couldn't get rid of will leave the taste of failure in your mouth.

If you allow your anxiety to be part of your performance, you will reduce its debilitating effects. After you've integrated your body and let the anxiety flow, shift your attention to the audience. Before you make your entrance, expand your body focus to include the entire audience and fill the performing space with your energy. If you have attuned your body to the size and emotional level of the audience, you will find that you will walk onto the stage at a pace appropriate to both you and the audience.

The principles for making an entrance from backstage can be adapted for more difficult entrances:

You are expected to give an after-dinner speech to a group that you know on a personal or business level, and to move directly from your seat at the speaker's table to the microphone. In this case, you are in a semi-performance role from the moment you enter the room until you leave your seat. That is, you are expected to be "one of the crowd" until you become the performer. Your role is more difficult than that of a professional politician or an out-of-town speaker in the same situation, who is expected to perform from the moment he enters the room.

Some of your entrance preparation will have to be done in the presence of the people who will become your audience. You can discreetly check yourself for physical stress and anxiety; you can assess the audience during dessert; but some of your pre-entrance rituals will have to be performed before you sit down at the table, and others adapted to the situation.

Be aware that you're balancing two roles at the same time: the performer's role, which requires distance from the audience, and the social role, with its expectations of bonding. Without this awareness, you're likely to get caught up in observing social customs and be unprepared for your performance. Or you may get caught up in your preparation and alienate those around you.

Balance is the key. If you are going to give a speech about the performance of the U.S. dollar in world markets, one of your dinner companions may ask you about the stability of the Japanese yen. Rather than getting deeply involved in a discussion of the yen as you might if you were only a business associate, you can say, "In general, I think we won't see much fluctuation until later in the year. Since I'm going to address that subject in my talk, I'd be interested in what your thoughts are." You can nod agreement, and say, "Hmm," or "Interesting," from time to time, without appearing to be rude or becoming deeply engaged.

You will want to switch exclusively to your performer's role just before you are introduced. Expand your bodily and mental focus beyond the table. Include the entire room.

The most difficult entrance is the non-entrance, the entrance in which the performer is present before some or most of the audience. Think of the pianist in a cocktail lounge. No matter how much rapport he may have established with his audience, each newcomer changes the energy content of the audience, and the piano player must adjust to that new level.

All of the above preparatory suggestions apply to such a performer, with one exception. He will not want to include a newly arrived couple in his body focus until they have settled themselves–until they have made their own transition from the street atmosphere to the lounge atmosphere and from being a couple to being part of the group.

In some business meetings, you may want to create a situation in which you arrive first so that you can control the seating and the group response to each newcomer. At other meetings, you may want to make an entrance after everyone else has arrived.

You will want to control the seating, if possible. The most power resides at the head of the table; the second most powerful position is the first seat on the right; power diminishes as the distance from the head of the table increases. At a round table, the most power usually resides with the person responsible for calling the meeting.

You will want to neutralize the seat directly opposite yours. Do not seat an adversary there, but rather to the right or left of that position. (If you really want to put your adversary off balance, place the floral centerpiece or coffee pot on the table so that he cannot see you directly.)

In some situations, you will want to seat advisors who are not full members of the group slightly away from the table; power can be given or taken away from them by their proximity to or distance from you. For example, an outsider at a board of directors meeting who favors your stand on an issue would be seated behind you and slightly to your right.

Whether or not you are making an applauded entrance, you will want to acknowledge the audience's presence. Our tendency is to practice the content of what we are performing without thinking in terms of the performance as a whole and the importance of building our relationship with the audience. Suddenly, it's our turn to speak and we haven't thought about how we get from here to there, the place where we're to begin speaking. Since many entrances are made from the side of a room, a dash to the podium gives the audience an excellent view of your shoulder, but not of your face, and you will appear to be hiding from or disregarding them.

Think of yourself as the host at a party. Performance conventions prevent you from greeting each individual as you would at a party, but you will want to include every individual by greeting the audience as a group. The conventions differ in different settings. Politicians and athletes may greet their audiences with gestures that say, "I'm going to win." The economist who is to speak on world currency markets, however, might find a grave smile the most appropriate greeting. A bow is expected in other situations.

If you are truly welcoming your audience, rather than thinking about how nervous you are, you won't have any trouble giving them a heartfelt smile, a smile that is appropriate both to your style and the occasion.

A true smile originates not in the lips, but in muscles in the center of the cheeks, about where some lucky people have dimples. This muscle center not only releases the corners of the lips, but the finer muscles under the eyes. Others respond to the smile in our eyes rather than the one formed by the movement of our lips.

We've all seen a parent who had a stern mouth and strong words, but laughing eyes when she reprimanded a child. We instantly understood that the parent's true feelings were in her eyes, and the rest was a response she felt obliged to give.

If you are applauded at your entrance, that applause is the audience's greeting to you. The applause says, in effect, "Welcome! We're glad you're here."

Your entrance smile and gestures are responses to the applause, as well as a welcome to the audience. They should be as broad, both in terms of physical expansiveness and length of time, as the applause.

Your entrance continues until your participation in the performance begins. One of the most important segments of an attorney's audience is the jury. They will be observing his demeanor at the defense table and beginning to make an assessment of him from the moment they are seated. All the elements of an entrance apply for the attorney, even though he entered before the jury did.

Each member of a panel of speakers assembled on stage should consider her entrance to continue until she begins her own speech.

If your presentation at a business meeting is halfway down the agenda, you will want to stay in entrance mode until then.

Treat your audience and yourself as you want your audience to treat you. I was seated in the front row of an outdoor performance of Kismet. When the 17-year-old ingénue made her entrance, I could feel a wave of emotion rushing over me toward the stage. It was so strong that I asked the person next to me, "What just happened?" Backstage, when I asked the performer the same question, she said:

> When I was working on the character, I realized that the first thing we knew about her was that her father loved her very much. So I just made her loved.

Excellent advice for every performer. How do you want your audience to feel about you? Make your entrance with the assumption that that's exactly how they feel.

Our world-currency expert wants his speech to be given serious consideration, which would require that he be respected. If this is his first speech, performance anxiety may trigger memories of every instance in his life when he was *not* respected. He will want to spend a few moments before his entrance countering those memories with other memories of how he felt when he *was* respected, even if these latter memories have nothing at all to do with economics or speeches. He will want to make his entrance in that mode.

Your work on your pre-performance inner emotional state will give you a naturally powerful posture and walk. Many performance students begin to make their entrance and then realize, to their horror, "People are watching me walk! How do I walk? I don't know how to walk."

Check your posture—but not in a mirror, because you won't have a mirror on stage. Instead, practice this simple exercise, which will give you an internal guide you can carry with you anywhere. After each step in this routine, adjust your balance and make sure your knees are flexed. (My son, the U.S. Army colonel, tells me that soldiers who stand at attention for any length of time with locked knees faint and have to be carried from the field.)

Adjust the contact of your feet with the ground so that each foot is carrying an equal amount of weight. Check your toes, heels, and both sides of each foot. (Personally, I have to make most of my balance adjustments during this first step.)

Bend forward from the hips. Place a finger in each open hip socket and raise your torso until the socket closes. Most people find this an unfamiliar position because they are used to walking with their heads in front of their bodies, rather than balancing their bodies over their hips and letting their legs carry the balanced body forward. Let your body ride on your hips.

Raise and rotate your shoulders; let them drop down and back so that the weight of your upper body is resting in the pelvis. You should now have a continuous line from the center of your shoulder down through your middle finger, your hip socket, and your ankle.

Drop your head forward. There are seven vertebrae in your neck. Roll your head up slowly, one vertebra at a time. This position also feels unfamiliar to most people. If you've been leading your body with your head, you've probably also been bending your neck and tipping the head slightly downward. A bent neck says, in body language, "I defer to you, whoever you are."

We often move our heads forward in order to "connect" with the audience, or to convince them of our argument. But an audience will unconsciously retreat from any connection with a performer whom they perceive as weak, and will not be persuaded to follow any course of action she suggests.

Even though an upright head obviously eases strain on the spine, I often hear the comment, "It feels too arrogant to hold my head so far up." "Arrogant" has its root in a Roman legal term, meaning "to adopt a child"; later, it came to mean taking for oneself something that belongs to another.

You are taking nothing from your audience when your head is balanced on a comfortably straight neck.

The audience wants you to be in control, to be powerful. The more often you practice this posture and your walk, the more reliable you will find your body to be. Your muscles will remember this position and will only need a quick reminder before you walk onto the stage.

CHAPTER FOUR

How to Deliver Your Message

My fervent hope is that you'll never arrive on stage without a message that you feel passionate about. Your opinions and beliefs are the reasons you've risked coming on stage, and the reasons your audience has come to hear you. In the ideal performance we could concentrate primarily on delivering that message, but learning any new discipline inevitably means that we get caught up in the techniques we're practicing. You may need to remind yourself several times during the process that you believe in this campaign, or product, or poem.

Good performance techniques form the setting that displays you and your material to best advantage. Each performer's message will be unique because each of us is unique. No two people will read a Rumi poem or sing a Schubert song in the same way. They will be interpreting that material from their individual personalities, life experiences, and belief systems .

Your message is yours alone, but the successful delivery of that message depends on learning performance techniques.

The preparation of your performance content is a creative activity. Your presentation of that content to an audience is a second creative activity.

The concept of perfection is inimical to creativity. We can practice our piano scales perfectly; we can do our math homework perfectly; we can type a manuscript perfectly. But when we try to carry over the notion of perfection to playing a Chopin sonata or developing a mathematical theory or writing the content of the manuscript, we are doomed to failure. In the latter instances, the emphasis *has* to shift from technique to communication, or the activity has no value.

Perfection has to do with objective measurement, and is an end in itself. Creativity can't be discussed in terms of measurement, for we are concerned with its subjective effect.

When we talk about creation, either the process or its product, we don't use the term "perfect." We don't say that a Chopin sonata was performed perfectly; we say we were moved by the interpretation or that the performer displayed great sensitivity. We don't say that a mathematical theory is perfect; we say that the theory is useful to explain a phenomenon, or we may admire its brilliance and originality. We don't say that the manuscript is perfect; we say that it raised several interesting points or that the argument was elegantly made.

An emphasis on perfection of execution may have been with us from the time the first soloist was chosen by a dancing community to represent them before their gods. But even then, the excellence of his dancing was seen as an indication of a more intimate connection with the gods, and not merely a personal attribute of physical prowess.

Perfect execution of a task became important as we moved from an agricultural to an industrial culture. A bolt that didn't fit its socket correctly was worthless, and a waste of material, time, and money. The system that was developed for educating industrial workers was based on the same perfect-or-worthless principle, and our children today are still graded on a right/wrong, correct/incorrect, perfect/imperfect basis.

But we are not in the business of producing hundreds of identical performances.

Each performance is new, created at that moment. The mistaken idea that we need to be perfect blocks successful performance. A potentially competent performer refuses to perform because "I'm not good enough." Or a performer fails to connect with her audience because she is standing between herself and them, making judgments on their behalf about how she is singing or speaking, dancing or walking.

An audience cares less about your material or how you are executing it than whether they are enjoying themselves. One of the highest compliments in show business is, "He could have read the phone book up there and the audience would have loved him."

I used that cliché myself recently when I congratulated a high school actor after a performance of a new play. She had been given the unenviable task of reciting a dozen lines that each began with a variant of "In 1813 . . ." "In 1872 . . ." and on and on. But she sounded so interested in what had happened in 1813 and 1872 that a recitation that could have been dreary became interesting to her audience as well. She demonstrated that the material is less important than the performance itself.

Perfect execution of the material is not essential to a good performance, either. A club owner said of a performer: "He can't sing very well and he can't play the piano very well, but when he walks out on stage the audience goes nuts. I book him every couple of months and always sell out."

If the value of a performance can't be determined by how good the material is, or how well it's executed, how can performers assess themselves?

We can't. Not by any objective standard of perfection.

But our internal subjective experience allows us to say, "That was my best performance ever."

The creative process can involve an altered state of consciousness called "flow," the perfect integration of intellect, psyche, and body. If we're not prepared for such moments, we may be frightened when they occur, but professional performers consider them the high points of their careers.

Professional athletes have been the most eloquent of any group of performers in describing the sensations they experience during flow: "the ball falls into the glove"; the opposing team "melts away"; "the arrow finds the target." One feels superhuman, able to exceed all normal limits. Training for this desirable effect is sometimes referred to as a Zen approach.

Allied effects are the ability to observe oneself performing—"I watched myself as I..."— and the ability to observe the entire situation and comprehend it in a different way—"I could see the entire field and everyone on it, and I knew where every player was going to move."

A sensation we sometimes experience is that of a split mind. We are able to monitor our relationship with an audience and adjust our performance in order to maintain the relationship, and at the same time be deeply involved in what we are saying. If our performance requires interaction with other performers, we are also able to monitor those relationships. Our judgments then are no longer "good vs. bad," but "this works" and "that won't."

Writers and actors report that the character takes over and acts in a way they hadn't planned. You can probably remember at least one time in your life when you were writing or talking and the words seemed to flow by themselves. Your logic may have seemed more intuitive than linear. The words may have surprised you when you saw what you were writing or heard what you were saying but, upon reflection, what you had written or said was sound.

No creative experience is entirely intuitive. You didn't forget the principles of grammar when those words seemed to come about by themselves. But we can learn to encourage those moments of complete integration. A place kicker may spend years practicing and executing kicks before he experiences flow, or he may experience it on his first kick and spend years practicing for the next one.

Another commonly reported aspect of flow is an altered sense of time: "I had all the time I needed to get under the ball," "I felt I was in slow motion," or "The ball slowed down."

Or we may experience time going by too rapidly. For example, you may find yourself making the fourth point in your speech with no memory of having made the second or third points; the elapsed time will have felt like two minutes, rather than six. Don't worry, you did deliver points two and three. If you had not, I guarantee you would remember that you hadn't.

If you're not prepared for this phenomenon, you may try to regain control by speeding up or slowing down your speech or actions in order to get in synch.

I have vivid college performance memories of feeling as though I were on a fast-moving train staring out the window in panic as station after station flashed by. Of course, I wanted to get off the train, and off the stage, as soon as possible. In retrospect, I know that as the performer I was the engineer and that, if I had my audience with me, we were all going to have a great ride.

The primary objective of a performance is to gather individuals together and hold them in a group throughout the performance. You plan to give a speech about county tax reform. You know what you intend to say and how you feel about tax reform. You've already gone through the first process, the preparation of your speech, but the audience is coming to your ideas and emotions with little if any preparation.

As you prepare for the second process, the performance of your speech, you will need to think in audience terms. Give them the time they will need to absorb each new idea. Practice pausing before and after each important point. Practice pausing between paragraphs, as you shift from one thought to another. Practice pausing after each phrase in long sentences.

If you want to encourage your audience's anger about the current tax situation, give them time to respond emotionally to your reasoning. Practice taking time for each illustration of tax inequity to sink in.

You are a writer on a book tour, planning to read from your latest novel. The town that you created for its setting has become so familiar you could draw a map of it; you know your narrator so well you could order breakfast for him. But both will be new to your audiences. Practice taking time as you describe the details of the setting, and as each new character appears.

When reading poetry, which is word and image intensive, you may want to pause after each image. Give your audience time to absorb an idea that may have taken you weeks to condense into two lines.

An audience will need time to absorb the concept behind a new software application, or the out-of-the-box thinking that went into a new ad campaign.

If you have accustomed yourself to using time on behalf of an imaginary audience, you will be able to adjust your timing to the size and energy of a specific audience.

Remember that you are responsible for carrying the entire audience with you through your performance and that the larger the audience, the slower its response.

The audience needs time to build up fear for the hero, to prepare themselves to vicariously swing through the air with an acrobat, to get the comedian's joke. They need time to understand what you are saying in your speech or presentation.

Use silence. Often a performing student feels he must fill every second with words, music, or action. Silence is a wonderful tool that you can use, not only for shifting your internal anxieties and focus, but for dramatic effect. Can you imagine a mystery film without silence? Or a trapeze artist who does not wait until we are breathlessly silent before she begins her most difficult feat? Or a comedian who does not use silence?

I watched a defense attorney's effective use of silence as he cross-examined witnesses for the plaintiff. Three times during the trial he turned away from the witness box as though his questioning were finished; three times he tucked his expensive shirt into his expensive trousers with a gesture that said, "Well, that part of the job is done," and walked toward the defense table. Each time the witness relaxed. She looked as though she thought she had also done her job well and that it hadn't been as bad an ordeal as she'd expected.

Halfway to the table, the attorney turned back as though he'd forgotten something. "There's just one other thing . . ." Silence. Then, in a tone that apologized for raising such a minor point, "When you said . . ." The questions and answers that followed were those that eventually decided the case.

Silence does not mean stopping, or resting.

The use of silence means giving yourself and your audience time to absorb your words and actions and letting them prepare for what comes next.

We also need to prepare both ourselves and our audience when there seems to be no "next," when the performance itself seems to have ended.

CHAPTER FIVE

How to Make Your Exit

We recognize the importance of our entrances and pre-performance preparations, but we give less thought to our exits and the post-performance period. We tend to say, "Hey! All I care about is that it's over, done, finished." That's true only if you never intend to perform again.

One of the performance aspects most difficult to learn is how to make use of the period of time between your last words or actions and your exit. If you believe that what you are doing or saying on stage *is* your performance, then of course you will feel that it is important to get to it and that there's no reason to hang around when you're finished.

The audience needs time to assimilate the entire performance. The larger the audience, the slower the reaction. The more strongly affected the audience, the slower the response. If any of their emotions have been deeply touched, they may need to regain their equilibrium in complete silence before applauding wildly.

How long, then, should the performer wait before making his exit? Is there a cue?

A young orchestra conductor says that after the last note of music he counts to 20 before he relaxes his body and turns to face the audience. If you decide to use that mechanical technique, you may find that 20 seconds feels like an eternity, and you are likely to fill that time with thoughts like, "How did I do?" "Did they like me?" "Did they hate me?" and/or "I must look like a fool standing here."

Notice that such thoughts are focused on yourself, not the audience, You will have withdrawn from the interaction, from the relationship.

If one person is distracted from a one-to-one conversation, the other person quickly recognizes the withdrawal and feels irritated, disrespected, embarrassed, even abandoned because of the lack of attention. We may say, "Where did you go?" recognizing that the other person is no longer present in the conversation.

When a performer withdraws from his audience to focus on himself, at some level of consciousness the audience feels abandoned. You can learn to judge your audience's emotional state, to feel the energy coming from the other side of the interaction, and to judge the appropriate timing for your exit just as you have learned to judge emotional readiness in one-to-one conversations.

During a casual conversation, you mention a dog you used to own. Your friend looks away, obviously disconcerted, then tells you her dog has been killed in a street accident. I trust that you would not walk out the door at that point. The previous conversation would end, and you would either try to comfort her or search for a topic that would allow her to leave the memory of the accident.

How much time will be needed for your conversation to return to its casual level? That could depend on how recent the accident was, the intimacy of your friendship, or whether she had a horrible day at the office. You have no way of knowing any of these particulars, but you can make a judgment about her emotional state and can adjust your side of the interaction accordingly. Because of the depth of the emotional interruption, you will take particular care with your exit, perhaps staying longer than you'd originally intended in order to make sure that the energy in your relationship has reached an appropriate level before you leave.

Audiences are made up of individuals who have had terrible days at the office and those who have had great days, those who've just had a fight with a spouse and those who've fallen in love and those whose dogs have died. Even if your speech contained a dog story and someone cried, each individual energy level is only one component of the communal audience. The communal energy level is the one you will use to determine when they are ready for you to leave.

The better the performance, the more reluctant the audience will be to leave. For the audience, leaving means not only the ending of an enjoyable experience, but their return to their individual lives.

As a performer, you will want to help your audience make that transition. Give them cues. In a speech you can sum up what you've said. As the late philosopher, Richard Rorty, advised me: "Tell them what you're going to say; say it; tell them what you've said." A folksinger can say, "For my last song . . ."

Some performers say, "Thank you," as a cue that the song has ended. This practice, however, sends the message, "Thank you for listening to little old me," and I don't recommend it.

Applause, if it's appropriate to the situation, is the culturally approved way for audiences to say, "Thank you."

Acknowledge their gratitude. Say, "You're welcome. Thank *you*," by smiling, even by bowing.

Americans are not used to bowing to each other, so practice at home. Think of the bow as containing three elements—a downward movement, a hold in place, and an upward movement. Begin by dropping your head forward; hold this position for a few seconds; raise your head with a smile.

For a deeper bow, bend slightly forward from the waist, letting your arms hang loosely; hold a few seconds longer than the first bow; unbend, beginning at the waist.

A full formal bow begins at the hips and may include an arm gesture that begins at shoulder level, then sweeps forward and down. Hold in place several seconds; unbend, beginning at the hips.

In general, the larger the bow, the longer you will hold it before returning to an upright position. Alternatively, if you increase the energy you're using for your movements, you can shorten the hold. Practice as many combinations as you can think of so that you'll have a repertoire from which to choose the most appropriate bow for the occasion and the audience.

Women use a curtsy instead of a formal bow. Dancers and some young girls still curtsy, as do debutantes in ball gowns and women in period dress. The unsuitability of modern dress has reduced its use for most women. However, should an occasion for a curtsy arise, practice by stepping backward with one foot. Lower the body by bending at the knees, with the back knee more deeply bent than the front one; drop your head; hold; raise the body from the knees.

When second bows and encores are appropriate, be prepared to use them. An audience won't give you points for being modest if you don't take a second bow; they'll feel cheated. Ease your audience's departure by increasing the time between your second and third (or more) reappearances on stage.

The length or volume of the audience response is not the best way to judge your reappearance on stage (or the success of your performance).

Be prepared to feel that no matter how much applause you receive, it will never be enough. Even if you're not performing as an athlete, the concentration and energy required for successful performance are so great that the applause will not seem sufficient compensation.

If you have just hosted a large party, the thank-yous of departing guests aren't enough compensation for the work and energy involved. You collapse on the nearest chair and review the events of the evening, preferably with a spouse or a good friend who has stayed behind to help clear up. "The Smiths seemed to have a good time." "The Joneses and the Browns really got along well." "The lasagna was a hit." The impressions, the vibes you received throughout the evening form your judgment about the party's success and are more reliable than whatever is said by the guests as they leave.

An audience may leave before the performer does. A bell rings, the class is over, students dash for the door, leaving the teacher/performer behind. Conference attendees may leave one lecture early because they want to hear part of another lecture. Commuters may separate from an audience and the performance because they need to catch a train.

In all these instances, as in the traditional applause-ending exit, the performer remains a performer until he has no further contact with audience members.

Obviously, the lecturer continues to lecture to the remaining audience if one or many people leave the room. The professional athlete may be interviewed after the game for a new audience; her performance is not over just because she's left the field. It's perhaps less obvious but equally important that the teacher remain a teacher and the attorney an attorney as long as they're in the classroom or courtroom.

A student performer who had just had her first successful performance left on a cloud. On her way home to make dinner for her husband, she stopped to pick up groceries. By the time she got to the check-out counter, she was depressed, and her depression didn't lift for a day or two. When I next saw her, she was quite angry with me, and rightfully so: "Why didn't you tell me that I had to come down slowly or I would go into a depression?"

All performers, not just athletes, can expect to be both exhausted and exhilarated after a performance. The professional establishes routines for coming down just as he does for getting up for a performance. Party. Celebrate with friends away from the performing area, but don't act as host. You've expended enough energy.

A performance continues for both performer and audience after the exit. A popular bistro singer complained that she couldn't come down after a set if she sat with the guests at a table:

> They don't understand. If I want to talk about the set I just sang, they begin to criticize me. But if I don't want to talk about the set or my singing, they won't let me just be myself.

No, the audience won't let a performer be himself. They don't want the performance to end. They will resent your piercing the veil of mystery if you initiate a discussion of the performance from your perspective. They want you to remain magical even after you've left the stage.

A young actress was preparing a role in Chekhov's *The Sea Gull*. Each time she came to a period in the text, her voice and energy dropped. In effect, she stopped her reading at each period. As she began to analyze what she was doing, she came to this conclusion:

> Oh! The performance never stops. The period is just a punctuation mark that makes the dialogue easier to read. But each sentence has to go on to another sentence, each scene to another scene, and even when the play is finished, you don't want it to stop. You want the audience to take it home with them and for it to go on forever and ever.

I attended a musical revue at which very few in the audience were younger than 60. On a very cold night, we aged ones actually danced on the cobblestones outside the theater on our way to the parking lot. Little clumps of strangers laughed together. We were unusually gracious as we waved cars to pull in front of us on our way to the lot's exit. I'm sure that most cars were filled with good humor all the way home and perhaps far into the night. I'm sure, too, that many of us urged friends to see the revue, for its run was extended twice.

Neither the director nor the performers could have predicted that effect, particularly on that age group. Their objective was to entertain, which literally means "to hold or keep among." Because they held us together so well, carried us with them into their dances, we could later dance on cold cobblestones.

I want to resurrect the value of that word *entertain*, which is so often used pejoratively, as if entertainment were somehow only the province of comics but not newscasters, of tap dancers but not teachers, of acrobats but not attorneys.

Whether your personal objective for your performance is to inform your audience about inequities in the county tax system, to win a wrestling tournament, or to coordinate changes in the corporate accounting system, your performance objective must be to hold your audience together so that they can mutually respond to your information, athletic prowess, or suggestions for change.

Separate your personal goals for a performance from the goals for the performance itself. If you are giving a speech on tax reform, your personal goals may be to achieve tax reform, to be respected and admired by taxpayers for your hard work and courage, to be acknowledged by politicians as a powerful taxpayer representative, to have your speech applauded and reported favorably by the press, to attract financial contributions and workers for your cause, perhaps to be elected to office yourself and then to move up to state and national office.

All the above are normal fantasies for the beginning politician, but unrealistic expectations for your performance. The professional knows that any one speech is only a small part of a process that will require organization, hard work behind the scenes, negotiations, and compromises.

You cannot predict and are not responsible for how your audience will use your performance. Audience members regain their autonomy after they leave a performance. They already have their own biographies, personal styles, and personal objectives, and those will determine how they use the performance.

If, at the end of your speech, you pass out a petition for the audience to sign, many more will sign than if you stood in front of the supermarket and approached them individually. But others in the audience, who may have joined in wild applause for your ideas, will begin to withdraw from the group at that point. For them, the performance was over as soon as they began to consider, as individuals, what they were signing.

If you ask your audience to sign up for committee work on tax reform, a minimum of 20 percent will later renege on their promises as the effect of the performance wanes. Again, behind-the-scenes work will be necessary to build a strong organization.

Even those demagogues who are able to incite audiences to specific actions cannot control them long-term without force. (Such audiences fall into a mob category, which have different objectives for forming than do other groups.)

Your objective for your tax-reform speech, then, should be developed in terms of how well you communicate your message and how you build your relationship with the audience during your performance.

As in any relationship, if the interaction between yourself and the audience develops respect for your views and yourself, they will want to continue the relationship, even if that continuity is not immediately apparent to you.

One performance is not a structure on which a relationship can be built; it is only a beginning. I had a voice student who was an organ major in a nearby conservatory. I wanted her to learn to sing well and perform well, and assumed that was what she wanted. But, no matter how hard I tried, she never achieved the vocal comfort I knew was possible, and she refused to come to the performance classes that I thought were so important. I felt as though I had failed her.

Several years after she graduated and moved away, I received a postcard from her:

> You thought I was studying voice with you. I wasn't. I was studying how you teach. It's taken me all this time to find an organ teacher who teaches the way I want to be taught, and I have to drive 100 miles for my lessons. Thank you.

That relationship was built through the use she made of my performance, not through the achievement of my personal objectives.

If your business objective is to have your audience purchase your office furniture system, the primary objective of your presentation is, nevertheless, to hold the audience together, to keep them with you as you move toward the contract. Even if your audience is one purchasing agent, you will obviously have your best chance at the sale if you maintain the connection.

Many concerns over which you have no control may enter into the final decision—family patronage, underbidding, a recently revised budget, a contract commitment made without your knowledge. You will certainly consider those possibilities when you're preparing for your next sales call, but a "no sale" this time does not mean the presentation itself was a failure.

Analyze your two objectives separately. Were you able to build a relationship that can be continued and that may result in a sale two years from now? Were you able to hold your audience throughout your presentation? If not, why not?

CHAPTER SIX

How to Create a Performing Persona

Most of us feel terribly vulnerable when we even think about standing in front of an audience. All those eyes staring at us, all those people sitting in judgment. We become aware of each physical flaw and character defect; in fact, everything about us seems to be defective. Childhood memories rise from our very bones–memories of being punished for being bad; memories of a circle of classmates jeering at us because we were strange or weird.

So how do we avoid exposing ourselves on stage?

We don't. We choose those aspects of ourselves that we want to display.

We all play many different roles in our lives. Each role provides us with certain benefits and brings with it certain responsibilities. Your role as a daughter is different from your role as an employee; both of those roles are different from your role as a customer. The relationships you establish in each of these roles have a different quality; you use your body differently, use different vocabularies, are prepared for a different level of intimacy.

As you and the other actor in each relationship change, so does your role. Your role as daughter changes as you grow from baby to adolescent to adult. If the mother-daughter relationship is to remain healthy, each adaptation of your role acquires new benefits and new responsibilities.

We know this before we can talk. We know when it's time to learn to dress ourselves rather than be dressed, and the wise mother learns to live with inside-out shirts and mismatched socks for a month or two.

A role only becomes superficial, a part acted rather than lived, when it does not change and grow. If your job does not acquire new benefits and new responsibilities over two years, you are likely to say you're at a dead end. If possible, you will look for a new job that promises to use more of your abilities.

But no job will use every aspect of your personality or ability. In your roles as son, college buddy, and parent, you will call upon different strengths and be willing to display different weaknesses.

We learn to shift from role to role as easily as we change clothes. My daughter was a scholarship student at a prestigious boarding school. At 14 she had two separate wardrobes acquired at flea markets: cashmere sweaters for Connecticut so she wouldn't look too poor and baggy cotton shirts for our New Jersey farming town so she wouldn't look too snobby. Today, as a finance executive, she loves getting out of her suit and high heels and into her work boots and hardhat when she travels to construction projects.

In each role we acquire we learn which aspects of ourselves are appropriate to display. We learn to play our roles through a combination of instruction, imitation, and intuition. If you are beginning to learn your role as performer, you will want to observe many performers. What are the qualities that you like in any performer? What are the qualities that you like in a performer in your field?

If you've just graduated with an accounting degree and are interviewing for your first job, you will want to assume the role of an accountant, not the role of an accounting student that you've been using for four years. What are the qualities you admire in accountants that you've known?

If you're going to give a lecture/demonstration on landscape design, remember your favorite teacher. Did you like him because he used his authority fairly? Did you consider him a leader? Did you respond to his sense of humor?

Any quality in others that draws you to them is a quality you possess and can learn to use in shaping your role. You may think that you have always been subservient but, if that were true, you wouldn't be able to recognize authority in others. Remember a time when you felt you were using your authority well, or when someone else complimented you on your fairness in a tough situation. Recall the inner sensations you had at that time; let your body reconstruct your posture at that moment. Did you seem to be taller? What was your relationship to the others involved? Were you unusually objective? Why? Had you prepared yourself for the situation in a specific way? Practice your lecture using this remembered posture and mindset.

Then repeat the exercise with the sense of humor you admired. You will find that your posture and walk will change with each new personality aspect. And that the process feels as though you were putting on a costume. Layer the costumes–first, the authority robe and then the humor robe. Reverse the layering. Which order feels more comfortable? Perhaps you feel at your best when the humor lies under the authority.

Repeat this exercise until you have added each quality you want to incorporate into your performing persona. Switch the costume order around. Feel free to throw some of the robes into the discard pile–perhaps your memory of having felt like a leader is not much different from your memory of your use of authority; or perhaps leadership works better than authority in the combination you've developed.

Here's a second exercise that could be helpful. Imagine a person who could deliver your talk as a comic routine. What would she look like? How old would she be? How would she walk? Talk? Think of as many details as possible so that your comic persona is a complete person. Imagine your audience and rehearse your lecture in this persona.

Notice that this comic character seems to protect you from audience judgment, as though you've put on a suit of armor. The character is partly you or you couldn't act her, but it isn't all of you. Using the same method you used to create the comic, create the persona that can best deliver your lecture and rehearse it again before an imaginary audience.

In both of these exercises you've created a persona from the inside out, choosing from qualities that only you have experienced, rather than constructing someone that you think an audience might admire. Both of these exercises are conscious, shortened versions of the subconscious method you've used to create other positive roles in your life.

As you gain confidence you'll find a lot of room for experimentation in your role as performer. Just as growth in the role of a son is important to a healthy relationship with a father, so is growth in a performing role important in future relationships with audiences.

Even if you've never danced in your life, think about your movement from the podium to the plants you're using in your landscape demonstration and your use of a pointer as being part of a dance. You might even want to take a few dance lessons to expand your performing role.

Your performing role can give you more freedom than any other. A performing persona will allow you to transcend not only the limitations you have placed on yourself, but those that others have placed on you.

We categorize people on the basis of any number of expectations, sometimes drawn from our own experience, sometimes from what our family, religious, ethnic, and political groups have told us, sometimes from the media.

We are all subject to categorization by others. If you have children, you've been told, "Everyone else's mother . . ." Your father had different expectations for boys than girls. If you played high school football, your team members, your coach, the rest of the high school,

How to Create a Performing Persona

the booster club all had expectations of your performance both on and off the field. If you're a banker, you're assigned a different role from a racecar driver. If you're a female judge or an African-American judge, you're subject to different expectations than if you were a male judge or an Italian-American judge.

Take a good look at the limitations you've accepted. "I'm too old to be a performer." You can create a performing persona that is not too old, or one that capitalizes on being elderly, one that will not only be accepted by audiences, but welcomed enthusiastically by many older people. "Men don't cry." On stage your persona can cry.

Assess the limits that even positive expectations have placed on you. A model-turned-folksinger complained: "I don't want to be just a pretty face anymore. I want people to see that I'm a creative person. I do have a brain. I want it to be recognized."

As I passed a young woman on the street, I thought, "What a pretty girl! I would certainly have remembered her if I had seen her before. She must be new in town."

Indeed she was new in town; she was my next appointment. She had come to work with me for several days because she wanted to change careers and needed to prepare herself for job interviews and for presentations to potential clients. During our first session we began to develop a persona who would counteract that first impression—"What a pretty girl!"—a persona who was no less attractive, but who walked with the authority of a competent woman.

Remember that audiences, above all, expect to be entertained. The limits they might have placed on you in a one-to-one interaction disappear when you become a performer.

A performer who had just turned professional reported:

> My last gig went really well—I knew I "had it" in two songs, so I'm getting really confident. But now I have a problem. I'm having trouble reconciling my performing persona with my real life. They're so different!

Well, yes! In real life she's a cancer survivor past retirement age who never married. On stage in retirement and nursing homes and hospitals, she's an "I-been-there-Baby" woman singing about good men being few and far between. In real life she has a new vivacity and sparkle and she looks great in her new red shirt and matching earrings. But she is wise to recognize that her performing role is only one aspect of her entire self.

We need to make a distinction between our performing roles and our social and business roles, just as we do between our parental and spousal roles. Professional performers who don't separate their roles become fodder for the tabloids.

Your audiences will want you to continue your performing role forever. The better you perform, the more completely will they feel they know you. Your responsibility to continue in your performing persona, however, ends when your contact with the audience ends for that performance.

You will want to remain in the performing role when greeted backstage or at a reception in your honor. But if you're a teacher who hosts your own child's skating party, you will want to do so as a parent even if the party includes present and former students. If you're an attorney, you probably already know that giving free legal advice at a party is not in anyone's best interest.

Be prepared for your family to have difficulty accepting your new role. It isn't the you they know. Parents especially, and occasionally spouses, may have trouble making room for this persona in their conception of their relationship with you. Until they realize that it is a performing persona only and that you can move freely from your new role to your old, familiar role, they are likely to fear that they will have to change.

My daughter was two when she first saw me on stage. I thought I had prepared her by rehearsing at home with the cane that I would be using to pound the stage, and by taking her with me when I was fitted for my costume. But I hadn't prepared her for the loss of her mother, who had turned into an operatic villainess. She was ill with a high fever for several days.

How to Create a Performing Persona

As children, most of us were told to restrain both our voices and our actions. We were told not to run in the house, not to speak unless spoken to, not to interrupt; we were toned down to fit into our families and classrooms.

An audience, however, requires that your voice, your gestures, and your energy be as large as they are, much larger than in any of your everyday roles—bigger than life.

You will want to fashion your role, and your actual physical presence, to fit the size of your audience. The tools and demonstration aids that you've used to teach one employee or apprentice gardener would not be appropriate in scale for a lecture to 50 gardeners. You will want to develop slides or other media that can be seen easily by everyone in the room. Your gestures, your voice, your persona will also need to be adjusted so that everyone can see and hear you.

Enlarging your voice doesn't mean shouting or projecting, but using more body space for your speaking voice. If you've ever tried to whisper in a great cathedral, you know how easily the smallest sound carries throughout the building. The size of the building, the materials with which it was made, and the angles with which it was constructed all contribute to magnifying sound. Sound waves leave your body and resonate (resound) as they bounce around the cathedral.

Think of your body as a potentially expandable cathedral or a unique musical instrument that can expand or contract to create a larger or smaller sound. Most of us use only a small portion of our bodies to resonate our speaking voices in our everyday roles.

Place your fingers lightly on your throat and swallow. The cartilage you feel moving up and down is your larynx (or voice box or Adam's apple). That's where audible sound originates in your body. With your fingers lightly on your larynx, say, "Hello," with a long, drawn-out "oooo" at the end. Did you feel the cartilage vibrate? Notice the size of your throat and any other internal space that you ordinarily use for speech.

To enlarge your vocal instrument, and therefore your voice, place your fingers lightly on your sternum, the bony plate directly beneath your throat. Imagine your chest as open space into which sound can travel. Say, "Hello" again, allowing (but not directing) the sound to fill your chest. Did you feel the sternum vibrate? Notice the size of your throat now, and add it to the chest space you've created.

Now place your fingers on your back along the lowest rib, and expand your image of open body space to include this area. Say, "Hello" again, allowing the sound to fill your entire torso. Did you feel your rib vibrate? Include your throat and chest in your new body space image.

You can learn to allow your voice to resonate throughout your entire body, from the top of your head down to your pelvis. Your voice is now issuing from that entire body, not just from your mouth. The larger the internal instrument you use, the larger the sound outside your body.

You may find that your speaking pitch changes as you open body space. Experiment with the pitch until you find the most comfortable range.

If you decide to change your speaking pitch you may find that you will need to change your pronunciation as well.

As children learning to talk, we usually imitate the pitch and pronunciation of our primary caretaker(s). Some of us, as we grow, never make the adjustments that would separate us from those early speech patterns and give us a more comfortable adult voice.

Because we learned to read by reading aloud, most people in this country still use far more muscles for reading than necessary. Because we learned to speak through imitation, most of us use more muscles than necessary to speak. If you use your voice a great deal–as a classroom teacher, for example–you may want to adopt standard stage pronunciation, which primarily uses the front half of the mouth to form words, and avoids, whenever possible, the intrusion of tongue or jaw muscles into the throat.

Use gestures when words are not sufficient to convey your meaning. How should we use gesture? Or, as I most often hear it phrased in despair, "What do I do with my hands?"

If you are giving a straight lecture, you may need little or no gesture to get your meaning across. Practice your talk without words; act it out as though it were a charade. Let the words run through your mind but let your body do the "talking." If you find any gesture that makes a point stronger, use it, expanding it to include the entire audience. Otherwise, let your hands hang loosely or rest them on a lectern.

The demonstration accompanying the landscaping lecture will need gesture. When you're talking to one apprentice you will usually use a finger or hand gesture to indicate a plant and where it will fit into your plan. Larger audiences will require, either live or projected onto a video screen, larger plants, a blown-up design plan, and a pointer. Practice with all these media until you're comfortable with them and use them only when needed.

Ideally, a pointer, or any other object that you hold, becomes an extension of your body. The student performer often grasps an object as though it were a shield and hides behind it. When using a laser pointer, a performer may forget he has it in his hand, and the little light circle dances meaninglessly, and distractingly, around the projection.

Let the object merge with your body; make it a part of your gesture; put it aside when it has served its purpose.

When you are practicing any stage movement, let the movement begin in your spine. Repeat the posture exercise in Chapter Three. Let your breath flow down into the abdominal cavity. Beginning at a spinal point about halfway between your waist and shoulders, let the muscles in your back raise your right arm above your head. Now raise your arm again, thinking of the movement as originating in the shoulder. Which method seems tiring or strained? Which seems to flow more smoothly? Move the point of origination lower and lower until your arm is moving from the base of the spine.

If, in the beginning, you feel uncomfortable with fully expanded movement, set restrictions. Practice your lecture without any movement at all—none in the head, feet, or hands. Now practice it again, allowing yourself to fill a space of six inches on all sides of your body. (Don't forget to use space above and below your body.) Gradually increase the allowable space until your body is no longer restricted in any way and you are comfortable with that freedom.

All the space in the performing area belongs to the performers. In my mid-50s I enrolled in a jazz dance course. When the instructor said, "The floor belongs to you," he opened up a new world of movement for me. He didn't mean that we were free to crash into other dancers, but that the entire floor was available for each of us and that we were free to claim the floor with each step.

Experiment with claiming space around yourself in a crowded elevator street, or hallway. When we retreat into ourselves in such situations, we get jostled because others don't feel any restrictions, any boundaries from us.

Many of the voice and body restrictions that we learned as children were associated with emotion. "Don't raise your voice to me, young man!" "There's nothing to cry about," "Control yourself." Those are only a few of the proscriptions that we heard as children. We complied with those orders either by closing down all outward manifestations of emotion, or by straining them through tightened throat and body muscles. By the time we become adults we may associate all emotion with a tight throat and body.

Shout, as loudly as you can, "No!" or "I hate you!" Did your throat hurt? Your back?

Get into good posture position, let your breath flow into the abdomen, and let your throat open as widely as possible. Remember a time when you were very angry. Let the remembered anger circulate through all the body space you can make available. Now say, "No!" many times, beginning softly and increasing in volume. Notice which muscles want to get in the way of the sound. Say, "No!" and "Yes!" alternately until both the emotion and the sound can flow freely throughout your body.

Pound a soft surface, like a pillow, as you say, "No!" several times until you can feel the anger flowing freely out your fist. Remember to let the gesture originate in the spine.

Say, "Yes!" several times, while you raise your arms to shoulder level. Repeat until you can feel your arms welcoming the entire world.

Emotion is the medium that carries the performer's message. What does anger have to do with performing? The emotion-blocking mechanisms that we develop early in life are not very good at sorting out which emotion to let through and which to hold back. If we've learned to block anger from surfacing in our faces or voices, we probably also learned to block any fear that might give rise to anger.

As a performer, you will want to have access to all your emotions because they are your direct links to the audience. Your audience may not know your songs, will probably not know the facts you present, but they are born with the same emotions as you.

In our culture, we often believe we are oriented to the bottom line and that facts are the only reliable bases for decisions. Human brains, however, are not as well equipped to work mathematical or logic problems as they are to make judgments based on intuition and experience.

An audience, as a unit, may not be able to comprehend quickly the finely wrought logical argument of a lecturer–that is, they may not be able to register and retain all the facts. They can respond immediately, however, to a lecturer's excitement about his final hypothesis, or about how she discovered her proofs, and be inspired to learn more.

An attorney asked me how he could get a jury to understand the complex financial instruments that led to the recent economic collapse. He said, "I spent days trying to work through them myself. Finally, one night at two a.m., I got it. So how do I reduce all the work I had to do into something a jury can understand?"

"By telling the jury that story. Tell them the process that led to your discovery. Tell them about the wrong paths you went down, and your frustration, and how stupid you felt. Give them a chance to empathize with you. They might not fully grasp all the complexities themselves, but they'll feel a connection to you and to your side of the argument."

In your landscape demonstration you will want to convey your excitement about good landscape design. If you love good design, you are likely to find poor design not only offensive to your aesthetic sense, but destructive to the land, and you will want to share those feelings as well. Within one lecture/demonstration we can see many appropriate opportunities to connect directly with the audience—enjoyment, distress, anger, fear of ecological damage.

New or raw emotion is too unpredictable to use in performance. Your audience has given you responsibility for the performance. They want you to be in control of every aspect. They do not want to see real blood seeping from the corpse on stage; they want to see what looks like real blood seeping from a body that will be able to take a curtain call.

If you've ever tried to talk while you were laughing or crying, you know that your words were unintelligible. You can, however, laugh or cry while you talk if you have distanced yourself somewhat from the original emotion, if you work with remembered emotion.

I've developed a general rule about using emotion in performance that says: "Tragedy requires one distance from emotion, comedy, two distances, and farce, three distances." A student who is an artist translated this rule literally (and, for herself, successfully) by measuring a "distance" as a foot-and-a-half.

What I mean by a distance, however, is a remembrance.

I had a friend who, through a series of strange coincidences, happened to see the *Hindenburg* crash. The flames, the falling debris, the bodies, the sounds were so traumatic an experience that he couldn't talk about it for weeks. When he told me about the crash a couple of decades later, he used it as another illustration of his strange ability to be present at historic events. Time and repetition of the story had given him so much distance that he could begin it this time during a light, laughing conversation.

Practice your performance using as much emotion as possible.

How to Create a Performing Persona

Cry, shout, rage, laugh, whatever–just let go. Remember, in as much sensory detail as possible, the mental images that triggered the emotion. Remember how your body felt in each instance. Did rage produce tension in your arms as though you wanted to hit someone? Did your laughter begin low in your body and bubble up through your throat?

Practice it again, using the imagery, physical sensation, and emotion that you remember from the first rehearsal. That's one distance.

If during the second run-through you're still vibrating with rage at the thought of fences being used in landscape design, because you hate, hate, hate fences, practice the fence section again until you are working only with remembered emotion.

If you decide that rage is inappropriate for this lecture, you may want to change your fence section slightly so that you can laugh at those who build fences. Then you will want to work with the memory of your rage during the second run-through–a memory of a memory, or a second distance.

Songwriters who sing their own songs, and poets and writers who are performing at readings, often distance themselves too far from their material. When a songwriter was agonizing over the loss of a lover, the raw emotion flowed freely. But when she is happily involved with someone new, the tearful song that she had written six months ago may seem irrelevant and her performance of it flat unless she revisits memories of the loss each time she sings it.

Remembered emotion is no less effective in performance than new emotion. In fact, remembered emotion can be more effective because you can adjust it to your audience's state of receptivity.

When you have mastered remembered emotion, you will have learned to control your emotions, not by trying to shut them off, but by using them as tools. A client had chosen to begin a performance of Abba's "Fernando" with the verse, "Now we are old and gray, Fernando." His rather old and gray audience began to laugh, so he played to that emotion until he could gradually bring them into his pre-conceived interpretation of the song as an anti-war protest.

CHAPTER SEVEN

How to Involve Your Audience in Your Performance

Projection seems to have become synonymous with performance.

It's the problem most beginning performers think they have: "I have trouble projecting." "I can't seem to project my voice." Invariably, their attempts to project voice, persona, or message to an audience have resulted in physical tensions that have made reaching their audience impossible.

Say a phrase in a normal tone of voice, perhaps, "Now is the time for all good men." Now imagine an audience of 50 or 100, and project the same phrase to them. What happened in your throat? Your back? Your abdominal muscles?

To project means, literally, "to throw." What muscles are you using to throw your voice? Many of us, when we try to project either our voices or our ideas, unconsciously shape our throats into weapons and squeeze as though we were shooting the words from a gun.

When I attempted to find a less physically damaging method of reaching an audience, I discovered the obvious: no audience wants to be shot at.

Not every member of an audience will be in a receptive state for the ideas you throw at them. Imagine a husband who believes his wife is unfaithful. He is unlikely to be receptive to much of *Othello* in that state of mind, and will probably resent, at some level, any Desdemona who throws or shoots her innocence at him.

How, then, are you to reach an audience?

Bring your audience into your performance. When I work with very young children I call this process "hugging the audience."

Uta Hagen, in her *A Challenge for the Actor*, pushes the imaginary fourth side of the set to the back of the theater to include the audience, rather than placing the fourth wall at the front of the stage as many actors are taught to do. In other words, she urges actors to mentally extend the stage until it fills the entire theater.

Faith Prince, in a Broadway revival of *Guys and Dolls*, used this concept beautifully. Every audience member, even those in the balcony, felt they were a part of the action, as though they were seated at a table next to hers. Or that they were passersby who stopped to watch and listen to an intriguing confrontation, ready to take her side, should she need them.

The inclusion performance method allows the audience member with the unfaithful wife to drop out when the going gets tough. He can sleep, make mental to-do lists for tomorrow, or think about why he doesn't want to participate in some of the *Othello* scenes, all without separating himself from the audience. He is free to tune back in at any time. The projection method, because it may feel threatening, can trigger his active resentment or physiological withdrawal. Whichever of these latter responses he chooses affects the essential groupness of the audience.

If they perceive an audience as threatening, beginning performers are susceptible to the phenomenon of physiological withdrawal. We tend to think of two protective responses to a threat—fight or flight—but there's a third that may be even more common—freeze. Our brains and bodies stop, as though frozen in time. We speak of our blood running cold. Our extremities are clammy. We have pulled energy away from body surfaces, but our hearts are beating wildly. This process seems not to conserve, but to use energy, for we're exhausted after the threat disappears.

Not too hard to see how the projection concept was born. "Wow, big, bad audience, you're scaring me. I'll just barricade myself inside this body and shoot my words out at you. Bang! Bang!"

The inclusion performance method expands your personal energy to embrace the entire audience. We use this type of energy every day to include and exclude people. We bond with some people, we give others a cold shoulder.

Most of us use this power unconsciously, but the performer will want to develop it as a tool. And a powerful tool it is!

We've all known people who light up a room when they enter. Much to my amazement, a workshop participant did the reverse. She dimmed the lights and slowed the electric fan when she practiced withdrawing her energy. The first time she withdrew, we thought the drop in electric power was external, caused by excessive demand during a prolonged heat wave. When it happened a second time, we asked her to experiment with energy withdrawal until we were satisfied that she, not the power company, was indeed responsible for dimming the lights.

An audience usually perceives inclusion or withdrawal in a performer at a subconscious level so is likely to talk of it in other terms, as in the following report on a folk-rock singer:

> There was a lot of sound up there, and you knew she was singing from her soul, but nothing got off the stage to me. Somehow she didn't look like she was on a stage. She looked like she was in a supermarket.

Most often audiences blame their alienation on themselves and not the performer: "I must have been tired, it was all over my head." Or "I guess it's me, I just don't understand classical music."

When we're included we may say, "He really got to me." "I love his voice." "She made the subject so interesting."

When we feel included or excluded by others in our everyday life, we focus on either our emotional responses (how we caused their reaction) or theirs (the reasons they act that way), rather than on the process itself.

Personal energy is measurable. Humans emit electromagnetic energy that has been and is being studied by social scientists (in, for example, work on "emotional contagion") and by researchers in the hard sciences, by the Department of Justice, the Russian KGB, and the U.S. Army Intelligence Corps. (I have an in-law who was involved with research in the latter group.)

Although most of us don't have the sophisticated hardware to measure personal energy, it is palpable—that is, perceivable by the senses. But not everyone perceives it in the same way. I talk of seeing the energy: I can see a corner of a room that hasn't been included; I can see the withdrawal line. Others say they can feel the withdrawal in their stomachs. Others report that their skin cools when they are excluded and that they feel warmer when included.

Two recent scientific studies have looked at the warm/cold effect of emotional response, and our language has many phrases that acknowledge its existence: "She gave me a cold reception," or "a warm reception," "He gave me an icy stare," "She has a warm voice," "I could feel the chill when I walked into the room." And, of course, all the sexual variants of "hot."

There's no right response, and it may be subtle. (Don't expect to dim the lights. I've worked with energy for more than 30 years, and I've never been able to repeat that phenomenon.)

To learn to work with energy, you will want to experience the process objectively, without any emotional load. Practice with a friend so that you can feel the effect of her energy, as well as getting feedback on the effect of yours.

Let your energy surround your partner. (I think of energy as a lariat that I can loop around people, even excluding and including individuals seated next to each other, but use whatever image works for you.) Try not to give him any movement or word cues as you then exclude him from your energy field. Alternately include him and withdraw from him until he can tell you exactly when you withdrew. I usually talk when I demonstrate this process so that my partner has a verbal reference point: "I felt the difference when you said the sky was blue." Then have your partner include and exclude you with his energy.

If you didn't feel a physical response, did you observe changes in your emotional response, either to yourself or your friend? Did you like yourself or him less when excluded? Or would you characterize your relationship differently when included? When excluded?

Some energy practitioners encourage you to release energy from different areas of the body—your head, your heart, your gut—noting any changes in energy quality and any changes in your body.

Such exercises can be good practice, but for performance purposes I suggest releasing energy from the back, which provides a wider focus and is more inclusive. Let it fill the space behind you, beside you, above and below and in front of you. You don't need to push energy out, just allow it to flow out. Don't try hard. Remember, you are just gaining conscious control over energy that you already use on a daily basis.

The volume of energy available to us seems to be inexhaustible. We can fill huge spaces with ease.

You can test this with your friend: expand your energy to fill a large area—say, three rooms—but don't tell her how far you've expanded. Begin to speak in a normal tone of voice. (Don't shout. Don't project.) Ask her to walk away from you and to let you know where the sound drops off. She will be able to hear your quiet voice in any area in which she's included in your energy.

Repeat the exercise without including her. She probably won't be able to hear what you're saying by the time she crosses the second room. She may not believe that you didn't change the volume of your voice, so switch roles—have her talk while you walk.

This is a great party game. You'll find it works through floors, walls, even down the street, as long as too much competitive noise doesn't intrude.

You'll find many other uses for controlled energy. Rather than withdrawing completely into yourself—freezing—when threatened, you can establish an energy barrier any distance from your body that feels safe. Use energy to fill the safety space around you. Use it to exclude adversaries and include colleagues.

On the other hand, if you feel yourself excluded by a person or group, feel free to respond by including yourself. Observe what happens when you include them in your own energy loop.

A female musician in an otherwise male rock band reported that she had trouble following the lead singer's beat because he was freezing her out so completely. After she tried including him in her energy, she reported:

> No problem with the music now, I can pick up the beat. What's so cool is that I can understand how his head works when I have my energy around him. He doesn't hate me, like I thought, so I don't take his attitude personally anymore. He's so bound up in his own stuff he can't get out of himself.

Be prepared, however, that in certain circumstances energy use can be tiring. A plaintiff in a civil court case described her experience:

> I was exhausted after four or five hours a day holding all those attorneys and the judge in my energy. But I kept them focused on me and what I wanted! And guess what? At the end of the second day the judge said he'd never seen a witness like me. He said I didn't stammer, I always knew what I wanted to say. I said, "I study performance." He said, "You mean that stuff works?"

In general, audience members that are not interested in your performance–the opposing attorneys in this case–absorb a great deal of energy.

Voluntary audiences, or involuntary audiences that you have interested in your performance, will help you with their own energy. At the same time you are filling the room with your energy, the audience is reaching toward the stage to include you in theirs. One of the great things about using the inclusion method of performance is that there is room for everyone's energy in the performing area and the total mass is greater than the sum of each individual's energy. When we hear performers credit the audience for their performance, they have used audience energy to augment their own.

Personal energy is the medium through which we pick up what others are feeling or thinking. Empathy, literally, "in feeling with," is established through this medium. We say we are in synch, in step, or in harmony with others when our feelings match those of others. When this match occurs, the emotion seems to be magnified and extended much as sound waves that find empathic resonance in a building are magnified.

The Japanese are adept at using *omaiyari*, or empathy; it's integral to their culture, as it is to many other cultures.

I had a Korean business partner for a few years. His English was terrible, so I acted as the front person for any business conducted in English. But I wasn't translating from Korean, a language that I've never learned; because of the empathy we had established, I was able to understand what he wanted to say from a few, badly pronounced words. We became so oblivious to the fact that we didn't know each other's language that one day he handed me a book to read, a book on nonverbal communication in business that I would have been delighted to read if it hadn't been written in Korean.

If you tune in to the energy that's coming from the audience, you can ride the waves. Some individuals in your audience may have withdrawn, some may be yawning, some may be emitting angry energy, but you will be able to feel the group energy, the composite of all the individual energy emissions, and that's the energy you'll want to work with.

Although common sense would tell us otherwise, many student performers find a positive, welcoming audience energy the most difficult to work with. They give various reasons: "They'll expect too much of me"; "I'll have to be better than I am"; "I feel too vulnerable."

Most beginning performers feel more comfortable dealing with coldness, anger, inattention. That's what they subconsciously expect, so over many years they have developed reliable responses—mollification, pseudo-cheeriness, withdrawal. None of these old responses are useful to the performer.

Use your practice partner again. Ask her to adopt a different attitude each time you practice entering the room, without using words or telling you which attitude she's using. She can pay no attention to you, be very angry with you, or adopt any other attitude she chooses, but one of her choices should be to radiate good will and a welcome as you enter.

Fill the room with energy before you enter it each time, so that you'll have a medium with which to pick up her energy. You'll find that, even if she's able to remain completely motionless and soundless, you will be able to feel her emotional response. Observe your reaction to each of her attitudes. Pay particular attention to your responses to her welcome, and write down any thoughts that arise.

The more you open yourself to your audience, the safer you will be. Although there are some exceptions—unhappy Philadelphia sports fans, for example—audiences in our culture don't throw things at performers. They seldom boo or laugh at performers unless they're watching a reality show that uses humiliation as entertainment.

The unwritten rules for most audience behavior guarantee more polite acceptance in a performer-audience interaction than in most interactions in private life. No young audience member is likely to yell at you, as your child might, "You're stupid. I hate you." No one is going to interrupt with, "You don't know what you're talking about," as a friend might.

The voluntary audience has not gathered in order to hurt you. Whatever else may be on their agenda, they are primarily there to be entertained.

An audience will be able to determine your attitude, as you were able to easily determine your partner's attitude as you entered a room.

How to Involve Your Audience in Your Performance

They will warm immediately if they sense your enthusiasm, but they will draw back if they sense a phony enthusiasm. They will accept any early anxiety because they will put themselves in your place and identify with it, but will feel far less comfortable with a bravado intended to cover your nervousness. (Notice how many times theater and music critics comment on a slow or nervous beginning but then go on to praise the performance.)

The more real, open, and vulnerable you are, the more your audience will trust you. I heard a clergyman begin a sermon by talking about his fear of presenting a difficult subject. Were we then nervous about what he might say? Of course. We were recalling past sins, wondering which would be the topic. But we were also immediately attentive–quiet, waiting, already involved–and because he was aware of his fear, yet had obviously decided to proceed, we knew that he was in control of his emotions and could be trusted. We could participate in his fear without being unduly afraid ourselves.

Had he not acknowledged the danger in a sermon on child abuse, but had launched directly into the subject, many in his congregation might have been frightened, but alone in their individual fears, and not able to face the issue safely as a group under his protection.

Had he apologized for either his fear or his message, he would have given his audience permission to disregard both as untrustworthy.

Think of all the mayhem you've seen on stage, in movies, and on television. In a good performance, you were involved with the victim or the perpetrator, sharing vicariously in his emotions. Most audience members know that the murder or beating they see portrayed on stage is not real, so they can safely discharge emotion. They can die without dying, kill without killing.

Vulnerability always feels risky, but the performer's risk-taking is one of his contributions to the audience. When you are open to your audience, you are saying, in effect, "I care so much about my message and about you that I am willing to take this risk." They will reward you for your courage.

The empathic abilities of an audience can be extraordinary. In a workshop at a homeless mission, we were involved in a walking exercise. Beau had been asked to embrace us with his energy, and then to walk with a message.

> "This stuff ain't no good. I seen nothin' but Beau's feet."
> "Yea, couldn't see his face, nothin'. Just his feet."
> "But my feets hurtin'," said Beau. "The shoes don't fit. I started out walkin', then all I could think was my feet."

We found that everyone in the workshop could point to the place in the walkway where Beau's attention switched from the exercise to his hurting feet. Instant belief in the power of energy transmission!

The flow in communication follows this path: imagination—emotion—energy field—emotion. If the basis of communication lies in sensory imagery, and a message is most effectively transmitted by emotion, and personal energy acts as the field through which both are transmitted, then we have a circular model for communication with an audience.

Imagine that you are presenting a line of kitchen cabinets to a potential buyer at his office. You have as demonstration aids a model cabinet face and a catalogue of line drawings and specifications. How do you convey the advantages of your line over others? How do you interest him in visiting a model kitchen?

Remember your own discoveries about the cabinets when you were first hired. Remember when you first opened a door and felt the strength in the hinges. Feel the firm resistance in your hands and arms. Remember the smooth slide of the drawer, your growing excitement over the quality of the fittings, and your research into their manufacture. Remember opening and closing doors and drawers in your own kitchen and your dissatisfaction with them, compared to these new cabinets. Remember your surprise when you learned that the price differential between the line you're selling and the kitchen you own was minimal. Remember your irritation, your anger at the builder who had installed schlocky cabinets in your house when he could have installed better-functioning cabinets like these.

Each of your visual, aural, and kinesthetic memories can be conveyed to the buyer through your memories of surprise, excitement, pleasure, and dissatisfaction. As he receives your input through the energy field you've established, he will be able to translate your emotions into his own sensory experiences with kitchen cabinets.

If I talk about cats, I have a mental image of a big white Angora cat named Jimmy. He was my first cat experience. No one in my audience will have had the same cat experience. They will not see Jimmy, as I do, when I say, "cat." Rather, they will remember their own cat experiences—a tabby, perhaps a sleek Siamese—and, in their own memory state, they will be receptive to what I have to say about cats. The more strongly and specifically I mentally see, touch, and hear Jimmy as I talk about cats, the more strongly and specifically my message will get through.

If I am telling a story about how Jimmy turned me against cats forever, the cat lovers in the audience may recognize the unfortunate experience, which in their view I should have gotten over. If I am telling a story about how I fell in love with Jimmy, the cat haters and those allergic to cats may roll their eyes and think me delusional. But both sides are more likely to forgive me for being on the "wrong" side of the cat subject if I am speaking from specific memories than they would if I made a general statement about liking or disliking cats.

If your practice partner is willing, try one more exercise with her. Read a paragraph to her. The material doesn't matter, just read it without any preparation. Then, take time to find a mental image for each phrase or sentence. See it, feel it, hear it—taste it and smell it, if you can. Read the paragraph again and ask your partner to relate any mental images it conjured up for her.

Or practice for your next performance by recording your presentation without any imagination. Just read what's on the page. Then create your images before reading it again. You'll find that your voice sounds so much more alive on the second reading that you'll be able to recognize any sentence or thought that wasn't accompanied by an image.

Many of the ideas in your presentation will not be as specific as kitchen cabinet hinges. If you are using concepts that don't evoke images, you will want to remember the incident that caused you to draw your abstract conclusion.

We use the word love, for example, in many different ways—to apply to a beloved person, to a community, to a vocation. In order to find an image appropriate to your use of love, remember the moment when you first knew that you loved that person, your new town, or your work. That memory will contain the emotion and images that will carry your message to the audience.

The most difficult message to sell is your new idea, your new product, your new design. Your audience has no experiences, no bank of sensory images into which they can translate your images because they are new. Imagine trying to explain a cat to a person who has never seen a cat or never even heard of such an animal. You would need to find shared experiences that were somewhat catlike in order to convey catness.

To involve your audience in your new idea, you will want to remember your own chain of discovery, beginning with your state of mind before the idea was born.

Describe the problem you were trying to solve, the need that existed. Describe the steps you took toward the solution, even some of the paths you followed that led nowhere. Lead your audience into repeating your discovery.

The human mind searches for patterns. We make sense of forests, stars, oceans, and our lives by fitting new information into patterns that we've already developed. As we experience new situations, we extract information. Sometimes the new information seems to fit exactly into our belief patterns, as though we had been waiting for that particular piece to finish the blue sky in a jigsaw puzzle. At other times, we think we've finished with the sky and are ready to work on the treetops, when we discover that a gray-blue piece belongs where we least expected it. The presence of a storm approaching from the left requires us to change our entire concept of the picture. Or, we may refuse to change our blue-sky image, become convinced that the gray-blue piece must have gotten into the box by mistake, and toss the puzzle out.

If you expect your audience to accept your message and incorporate it into their lives, you will want them to accept its validity and usefulness. Before they can do this, you yourself must be convinced. Communication in any interaction is preceded and followed by opinions on both sides. If you say that the moon is full, I may accept your statement, or I may tell you that the moon won't be full until tomorrow night and show you an almanac. Every real statement (as opposed to small talk or chitchat) contains an opinion.

Believe in your entire message. Your conviction, your commitment will be transmitted just as you picked up the attitudes of your practice partner. Your opinions may not change the judgments of everyone in the audience, but if you don't believe everything you say, how can anyone else?

A songwriter explained why he had inserted abrupt rhythmic changes into a new song: "I didn't want the audience to get bored . . . Oops! Maybe *I* was getting bored . . . Maybe I need to look at the lyrics again."

You believed in your message when you first began to prepare your presentations. Your words were flowing from little mental film clips—you were seeing and hearing images as you wrote. Then during the refining process, as you moved paragraphs around and corrected grammar, the images, perhaps even the message, got lost.

In this new creative process, the preparation of your performance, you will want to call up the images again, this time to create an entire mental film or video in which one image flows into another with conviction.

CHAPTER EIGHT

How to Handle Performance Disasters

Our anxiety symptoms are usually at their height just before we go on stage. Disaster scenarios shiver through our minds. Our mouths go dry, our palms sweat, and our knees shake.

You will need some amount of anxiety in order to give your best performance, but if one or more symptoms are drawing your attention away from your preparation, you will want to reduce them to a manageable level.

Take care of yourself. You may find that your energy is low, or that you feel somewhat depressed 24 hours or more before a performance. Don't try to push through for a heavy rehearsal. Your body knows what's going on and is conserving energy.

You will not want to put heavy demands on your digestive system immediately before a performance. If you're performing after dinner, make lunch your primary meal of the day and include a good protein. If you're performing in the early afternoon, make breakfast your protein meal.

The last meal before a performance should be light. Eat comforting food. The foods we find most comforting are often those associated with childhood and/or illness, so they are likely to be easily digested. Soup is a good choice if it's not cream-based. You will want to avoid dairy products or any other class of foods that may generate mucus in the throat. Avoid citrus fruits, pickles, and other sour foods; they tend to be drying. Avoid nuts, crackers, chips–pesky bits can lodge where, although no toothbrush can find them, the sound vibrations from your voice will set them free.

Go with anxiety symptoms, rather than fighting them. If you have experienced any of the following symptoms before or during a performance, practice their remedies at home.

In order to counteract a dry mouth, many performers carry a thermos of warm, weak tea sweetened with honey. Some like to add lemon, others avoid lemon at all costs, so experiment at home. Many venue contracts offer a selection of beverages that will be placed on stage for performers and/or in their dressing rooms. Other venues will provide a carafe of water and glasses. Ask that the water be at room temperature.

If liquids don't help, try this suggestion from Eloise Rispad in her *A Soprano on Her Head*: instead of fighting your dry mouth (and becoming angry at yourself because you're not succeeding), let your mouth become as dry as possible. You will probably find that you were very near a dryness threshold. Just beyond that threshold, saliva will begin to flow again.

We seldom succeed when we try to overcome a natural physical reaction by brute force or willpower. Instead, let the reaction run its full course. Your body is equipped with mechanisms that are triggered when your emotional reactions exceed safe limits. These mechanisms exist to maintain physiological equilibrium. Trust them.

If your voice seems shaky, squeaky, or threatens not to work at all, it's been tied up by muscle tension in your throat and chest. Let your shoulders drop; let your entire body rest in your hips; let your anxiety slide down into your hips, too. Breathe slowly into your abdomen several times.

Should you have vocal problems during a performance, you will need only a few seconds to drop your shoulders and take one slow abdominal breath. Use these silent seconds as a dramatic pause, or to suggest that you need a moment to answer a question or to think through what you want to say next.

You can calm shaking knees by rehearsing our posture exercise. Grounding your feet, with knees flexed, as we suggested in that exercise, is especially helpful if your knees begin to shake when you're on stage.

If your hands are trembling, rehearse the gesture exercise in Chapter Six. If you feel them shaking while you're already on stage, drop your shoulders.

Our appendages become a problem when we've detached our minds from our bodies, when our heads are whirling with anxiety and we've lost any conscious connection with our hands and feet. Take a moment to think about the relationship of your spine to your hips. When you can feel that connection, take a few steps by moving your legs from the hips; open your arms wide from the spine; raise them above your head. Your objective here is integration from the top of your head to the ground.

One of our major fears is that we will forget what we intend to say. Not all of us remember in the same way—some remember best what they hear (auditory memory); some remember best what they see or read (visual memory); some remember best through physical activity (kinesthetic memory).

The most striking example of kinesthetic memory that I know is that of a prep school girl. The night before an exam she took one page of paper to the library. As she studied, she wrote notes all over the page until it looked like a giant ink blot; then she crumpled it up and tossed it into the wastebasket on her way out of the library. She remembered almost exclusively through the act of writing.

You may want to use all three memory methods when you prepare for a presentation. Write what you want to say; read it aloud into a tape machine; then listen to the tape. If you've created the internal videotape of images that accompanies your presentation, you will be able to remember your most important points.

You won't want to memorize your presentation exactly, unless you're acting in a play. Written communication is usually much more formal than spoken communication–what may read well on the page is likely to sound stilted when spoken aloud.

Our expectations of spoken grammar are much looser. If the audience has become involved in the presentation, they will accept pauses with the assumption that the speaker is giving thoughtful consideration to what she will say next; they will accept an "uh" here and there while the speaker searches for just the right word; and they will accept run-on sentences and even sentences without a subject.

If you find during your presentation that you've skipped an essential point, you can bring it in later. You can probably count on one hand the lectures you've heard since you left school that could be taken down in outline form. Such lectures are useful to students taking notes for an exam, but are probably less memorable than others that went off on exciting tangents.

The differences between writing and speech mean that you will not want to read your presentation to your audience, unless you are an author or poet. When reading, our tendency is to narrow our personas to book size. Back in the 70s, I attended a poetry reading by a well-known writer. She appeared to be a waif who had wrapped her thin body apologetically around the microphone. By shrinking both her persona and focus, she had drained much of the power from her war-protest poems.

A performer who reads aloud must focus on the book from which he is reading and at the same time use a broader focus to include the audience. This sounds like patting your head and rubbing your stomach simultaneously, but the process can be made simpler if you bring your audience into the book with you.

For other performers, if your presentation will include numbers, quotations, or any other material that requires accuracy, write them in large characters on 4" x 6" cards. When you're ready to compare December's sales figures to those of five years ago, pick up the appropriate card and read from it. If you plan to quote directly from

How to Handle Performance Disasters

an issue of the *Wall Street Journal*, print it out in large type so that your eyes will not have to adjust too narrowly from your audience focus. Treat these materials as you would any other demonstration material—first, practice with them; then, during your performance, use them consciously and deliberately on behalf of the entire audience.

Use technology as a tool, rather than as an end in itself. Another common source of anxiety for beginning performers is the use of a microphone.

Check beforehand what type of amplification will be used. Body mikes were originally designed to be clipped to a suit lapel—a position fairly close, but not too close to the throat. This is still the type of body mike you are most likely to encounter. Women will want to choose clothing that provides an attachment point that is similarly situated, such as a pocket, or at the second button of a blouse or shirt.

If a standing microphone will be used, or one attached to a lectern, and you have planned to move away from the lectern for any reason, make sure that you can remove the mike from its stand and take it with you.

In this case, you'll be working with a handheld mike with a long cord, so you'll want to practice at home. Tie a long piece of rope or string to a chair and tie the other end to a long-handled spoon. Practice moving from the chair to the easel or projection screen you plan to use, and then move back again to the chair, using your free hand to gather the rope out of your way.

Because of the cord, a handheld mike requires the use of both hands, so if you're using a pointer or any other object in your demonstration, you'll want to remember to position it at your demonstration site before you begin your presentation. Practice at home with both your spoon-and-rope microphone and your demonstration materials.

Whatever type of amplification is used, arrive at the performance site early enough to check your voice with the sound system before the audience arrives. Expand your energy to fill the room; speak a sentence or two with your expanded voice.

If you speak only to the microphone, you will narrow your energy and voice focus and exclude your audience. Expand your energy and focus to fill the room and let the microphone do its job. Ask someone to stand at the back of the room to make sure you can be heard clearly there, and to make sure that the bass and treble settings are right for your voice. Adjustments can be made either at the system controls or by changing the distance between yourself and the microphone.

Radio, recordings, and television require a different approach to your audience. You will use a radio or recording microphone differently. Although your audience may number in the tens of thousands, each member of your audience will be listening as an individual. You will want to imagine that audience member somewhere beyond the microphone and to include her in your energy loop. Positioning her in the control booth usually works well but, if possible, you'll want to experiment with her placement and have the results played back to you.

If you've been disappointed with a recording of performers you've heard live, they were probably performing to the technology rather than using the technology to communicate with an imaginary listener.

A television camera works the same way. If you assume that the camera is the audience, your viewer won't be able to reach you from his living room.

A former client called to report on a TV audition:

> We'd only worked together on live lectures, and at first I didn't know what to do about pulling the audience in with my energy. But I'd made friends with the cameramen when I walked in, so I used them as my "audience" and it seemed to go well. I got a callback, and they said they're thinking of giving me my own show.

The more high-tech your presentation aids, the more carefully will you need to check out in advance the equipment at the presentation site.

How to Handle Performance Disasters

Don't assume anything; check out everything. If you're bringing some equipment with you, is the site equipment and cabling compatible with yours? If you're giving a daytime presentation, can the site lighting be adjusted appropriately so that your screen can be seen? (Don't forget to check on whether any windows have light-blocking curtains or drapes.)

If you'll need assistance, either bring your own or plan to rehearse with the site technician. If you're using tapes, slides, or discs, bring back-ups. Bring any repair tools you might need.

No performer ever feels that they have done enough preparation before they go on stage. Much of our pre-performance anxiety can be summed up as, "I'm not ready. If I only had another day (or another week or another month), I would be fine."

No, you wouldn't. The only performers who feel ready to perform are those who've been acting in the same play or touring with the same music for months and have to fight against boredom and staleness.

Reading readiness doesn't mean that a child is ready to read perfectly, only that he is ready to learn to read. Whether you are preparing for your first or your hundredth performance, you only need to be ready to learn from it.

I will confess here that the reason I rail against perfectionism is because I have to fight it in myself. I began to accept the concept of good enough when my desire to be perfect had put me in a position that even I could see was ridiculous.

I had been doing research for a book on American dance when my longtime writing mentor telephoned. I told him how many books I had read on Amerindian dance, and how discouraged I was that I still didn't completely understand some of the subtleties or some of the tribal distinctions, and I had this deadline to meet, and Indian dance was only in the first chapter.

He interrupted my babbling with, "How many pages are you giving to Indian dance?"

Silence on my end of the phone. I managed to squeak out, "Three."

He said something about "good enough," but I'd already gotten the message.

A complete list of everyone's fantasies of performance disasters would be endless. The most common performer's nightmare is some variation of finding herself on stage, naked. That's not likely to happen.

On the other hand, accidents do happen. One of the reasons that audiences like live performances is because accidents happen. We pay close attention to all performers, and lots of money to professional performers, because they are taking risks and we in the audience are not. Audiences are, therefore, very forgiving of what performers think of as disasters. In fact, a lively little market exists in bootlegged tapes of famous performers' mistakes.

Do we love performers any the less because they played a wrong note or stumbled over a line? No, we love them more because they have proved themselves human and have allowed us to identify with them.

During the American Bicentennial, I saw a revival of this country's first indigenous opera. The performance was double cast, and the bass on that night was a big man, well over six feet tall. In an early scene he was supposed to take his coat from a peg on the wall, put it on, and then, after a couple of lines, exit. Unfortunately, the coat on the peg that night belonged to the bass in the other cast, a small man, which became obvious to us all as we watched our bass try to struggle into it. He gave up, held the coat out in front of him and ad-libbed a line about its having shrunk in the wet weather.

I could feel the audience drawing together for the first time in what had otherwise been a less than first rate performance. We laughed, we applauded, and we enjoyed the rest of the evening far more than we would have without that "mistake."

CHAPTER NINE

How to Become a Star

Those people we call stars are using their personal energy to the fullest.

We say that a politician has charisma or a magical something and we predict that "He'll go far." We say we are drawn to a film star, that we can't take our eyes off her. We say about a teacher of 20 years past, "He changed my life," or, "She turned me on to chemistry." We may explain the phenomenon to ourselves by saying, "I like what he has to say," "I love his smile," or "She knows her stuff." In actuality, we are responding to the star's inclusion of us in his world, if only for a brief moment. We became fans.

A lovely young blues singer in our town died after a long illness. I identified with what I heard others say: "I don't know why this is effecting me so much. I don't really know her, but I've heard her sing."

We felt as though we had lost a best friend, even though many of us had never spoken to her. But we felt we knew her because she had sung for us, not to us. She had brought us up on stage with her and had sung the blues on our behalf, and our lives were diminished without that experience once or twice a year.

You have the right to perform whatever you believe in. The nature of the interaction with an audience gives the performer enormous power. Can that power be misused? Of course, as can atomic fission, electricity, water, fire, or any other source of power.

The issue for most beginning performers, however is not the abuse of power, but their right to use their inherent power. If you believe in your message, your product, or your song, then you have the right, perhaps even the duty, to share that belief with others.

I attended a lecture on evolution given by a young mother whose formal education was in the fine arts. She isn't an expert, as we usually define that word. She doesn't have any of the correct academic credentials, just a love of the field. She takes courses and seeks out mentors; she reads voraciously. She has begun to write about evolution and to lecture on it because she wants everyone to share her enthusiasm for this theory and to recognize its importance.

A young woman was forming a consulting company that would specialize in market research on the female consumer:

> I was talking with my partner about what our policies would be when we got big enough to hire more people, and we talked about salaries and I realized that most women don't know how to negotiate their salaries. They're getting paid $30,000 and they expect their boss to say, "Your skills are worth $50,000. Here's a $20,000 raise." Even *I* wouldn't do that! So I'm giving a seminar for women on salary negotiation. I've reserved a room, and I'm placing an ad, and the newspaper's going to interview me, and I'm going to do it!

A freshman telephoned me after her third callback for the lead in the high school musical:

> It went so great! And I figured out why. Because while I was up there, it was *my* part! And it doesn't even matter now whether I get it or not . . .well, it *does* matter. I mean, I'll be upset if I don't get it, but now I know what it feels like to have a part be mine.

Each of these women claimed a subject, an idea, or a role as her own. Each believed in it so strongly that it became hers to share with others, even though each of them also knew that the subject, idea, or role was not exclusively hers.

We usually think of a claim as a legal right to property that excludes all others, but we've learned that when a performer claims space he is sharing it with his audience, rather than excluding them from it. The same paradox applies to performance material.

I've noticed, as I research popular music, that some songs are revived by different singers about every ten years. Cole Porter's "I've Got You Under My Skin," for example, was written for a 1936 Jimmy Stewart film. It was featured in at least two other films, appeared eight times on *Your Hit Parade*, was recorded with great success by both Dinah Shore and Frances Langford, and became one of Frank Sinatra's signature songs.

Although the composer held the legal rights, Sinatra's performance of the song allowed him to claim it in another way. When many of us remember that song now, we hear it as Sinatra sang it, but who knows when another singer will make it her own.

No matter who wrote the material, the performer is its communicator, the one who brings it to life. To see a Shakespeare play is a completely different experience from reading a Shakespeare play; to interview a candidate for a job is completely different from reading his resume.

Each actor, each singer, each salesperson, each job candidate is unique because each of them has lived a life that no one else has lived. I had long theorized that to have two persons sing the same material in a performance class would be a useful experience for both the singers and their audience. When I had the opportunity to test this theory for the first time, however, I worried that the audience would be bored. Two students had prepared *"Frauenliebe und -leben,"* a cycle of eight songs about a woman's love and life. Eight songs, sung twice on the same program? But the singers' life experiences had been so different that, although they sang the same notes, the same words, the same rhythms, they seemed to be singing entirely different songs.

When we claim the part, the song, the product, the job as our own, we begin to fall in love with it. We nurture it, care for it, give it our full attention. When we focus on our material, we find the courage to live through the anxiety of performance, and the drive to learn how to perform it well. When we love our material enough to perform it, it begins to drown out the voices in our heads that say, "You can't," "They'll laugh," "You'll make a fool of yourself."

If you've been able to claim your material, your performing space, your audience's attention once or twice, why not go further? Why not claim stardom, as well?

Not everyone wants to be transported into a life of limousines, paparazzi, and million-dollar fees. Not everyone wants to deal with the business part of show business. But what you have to say, your own unique message, can have a great impact on many people.

Perform as often as possible. Schedule a second performance before you've completed your first. You'll find that you will approach the first performance differently if you know that there will be another one. The first performance—and the second, and the third, if you continue to schedule ahead—then becomes not an end in itself, an exam that you either pass or fail, but a stepping stone to becoming a performer.

As the exhilaration of the first performance fades, you will probably feel depleted of all energy. Give yourself a day free of analysis, except for mentally filing away every audience comment you received.

The following day, review your performance, beginning with your preparation immediately before going on stage. Did you remember to fill the room with energy? Could you feel audience energy before you walked in? Did you lose your focus on the material? When? What thoughts shifted your focus? Were you able to include the entire audience throughout your performance? When did you lose them?

How did you get them back? Did you feel comfortable acknowledging applause? Were you uncomfortable at any time? Why?

Some of your answers to these questions will give you very practical remedies immediately. If your feet began to hurt after five minutes, consider wearing different shoes when you perform, and/or review the posture exercise.

Other answers may require more thought and practice. For example, you may have had a flash memory during performance of your traditionalist grandfather saying, "Children should be seen, not heard," and then felt your face stiffen and your throat close. You will want to consciously deal with the fact that you are an adult now. Perhaps you can exorcise his voice by imagining your grandfather as your audience when you rehearse for your next performance.

After you have extracted as much information from your memories of the performance as possible, compare the audience comments you received with your own assessment.

A good friend may have told you that you didn't seem as comfortable with the end of your speech as when you began. His observation may well coincide with your memory of being distracted by those painful shoes at that point. An audience comment such as, "I loved your story about the boss from hell," may remind you that you told that story from a very strong mental image.

On the other hand, don't be afraid to discard audience comments after weighing them carefully. An elderly gentleman may have told you that he not only disagreed with your point about the boss from hell, but thought your language was inappropriate. He got the point if he disagreed with it, so your delivery of that story was a success—both the pro and con factions heard what you were saying. Don't shy away from healthy disagreement, but consider which response is more important to you and whether modifying the story slightly would dilute its effect.

Now is the time to prepare for your next performance. Make notes about what to check or do beforehand, how much time to allot for each pre-performance activity, what to eat (or what not to eat), what kind of clothing might be more suitable for your onstage persona and/or more comfortable.

Don't neglect your post-performance routine. If you didn't end the day with a feeling of satisfaction or were depressed in any way, plan for your next post-performance celebration differently–more (or fewer) people, more (or less) food, a bottle of wine (or no alcohol), a longer wind-down period, less time spent at the reception where you were expected to remain in your onstage persona. You'll learn through trial and error what works best for you.

Set a new objective for your next performance. Choose the least frightening or risky possibilities for expansion.

Perhaps you want to use more gestures next time. Set a modest goal, perhaps to add one-third more arm and hand movements than you used last time. As you practice the gesture exercise, exaggerate each gesture. Make each one too big. If you feel that opening your arms to welcome the audience is appropriate, open them too wide; imagine that you're Liza Minnelli at Radio City Music Hall.

Practice the exaggerated gesture until you begin to feel comfortable with being a star, then decide which size gesture is appropriate for your audience. Err on the side of too big rather than too small when making this decision.

One new risk for each performance is sufficient, but other areas to use for expansion are space, voice, emotional expression, and energy. With the exception of energy, practice using too much just as you did with gesture.

If you have learned to fill the entire space with your energy, expansion in this case will involve density rather than size.

Observe an interaction in which you're not very interested, or remember a recent conversation. Perhaps a friend has discovered the perfect fabric for recovering her sofa and describes it in great detail. Sense the density of the energy you're using. You are probably using sparse or thin energy, just enough to keep you awake so that you can say, "Um-hmm," now and then.

Observe (or remember) an interaction in which you're quite

excited. Perhaps you've just played the tennis match of your life, and are describing it stroke by stroke to your friend. Sense the density of your energy. You are probably using concentrated or thick energy.

Performers often describe extremely concentrated energy as visible— "It looked like blue electricity playing around the stage," or "She gave off sparks."

Experiment with the density of the energy you emit when you fill a room. Observe your body and emotional state at different levels of energy intensity. Practice using dense or sparse energy in your usual daily activities.

A rock musician says:

> Sometimes I concentrate on someone at the back of the room, and it always works. After the show the one I picked out comes up and tells me how great I was. Last year I was at a concert, and I got myself invited up on stage the same way. I just focused on one of the band members until he asked me to come up and join them for a number.

I can't promise those exact results, but you will see a difference in how you're treated when you use a star's energy.

You will soon find that you are watching others perform in a new way. Singers, newscasters, dancers, and attorneys all become your teachers. You now understand what they are doing and why. You begin to identify with the professionals; you're part of the same club now.

Have fun when you perform. To perform is an intense experience, about equal to flying a fighter plane, or so a pilot told me. He said that fighter pilots are not only different from other people, but different from other pilots, and that he can pick them out from a crowd. They've learned to tolerate high levels of risk. They've gained confidence from each risk taken, and relish any new challenge.

Performance is learned behavior, just as flying a fighter is, but the performer doesn't need a multimillion-dollar machine to learn confidence in herself, just a few people with whom to share her message.

Learning to perform isn't easy; if it were, the rewards wouldn't be as great or the experience as fulfilling.

In an ideal world, we would all have been encouraged from birth to perform, and those who enjoyed it the most would have been encouraged to consider performance as a career.

Although we have been born into a less-than-perfect world, each of us has a unique story to tell, a song that has never been heard before, a dance that has never been seen. Each of us, without exception, can learn to speak up.

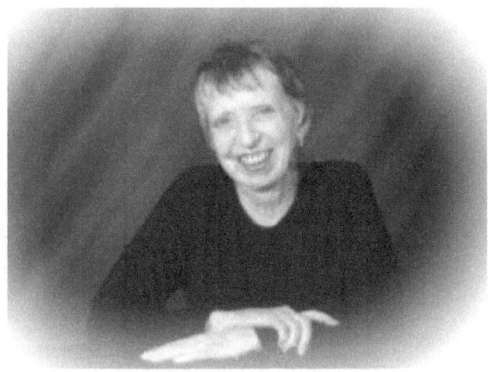

CAROL ROAN holds master's degrees in music from Indiana University and in business from Columbia. She began performing professionally as a singer at eighteen. Critics were soon commenting on her stage presence, which became the focus for her later research. She developed a method for teaching others how to communicate with an audience, and taught the first stage presence course in the country at the New School of Music in Philadelphia. Since that time, her clients have used their training in venues ranging from the Metropolitan Opera stage to boardrooms, courtrooms, and classrooms. Carol is the author of *Clues to American Dance* (Starrhill Press) and co-editor of *When Last on the Mountain: The View from Writers over 50* (Holy Cow! Press). She currently teaches voice and stage presence in Winston-Salem, North Carolina.

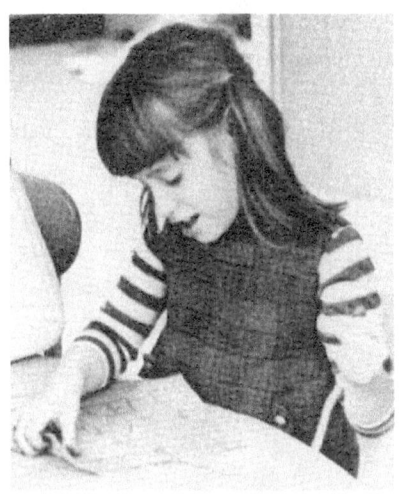

Cover designer **VICKI LATIMER ROAN** was once sent home from nursery school for painting her arms, legs and face. She's progressively improved upon staying inside the lines. Since opening her own design studio, Vicki has focused mainly on print projects, including logos, business collateral, packaging and custom patterns. Moving to Winston-Salem, North Carolina in 2007, she lives and works in the West End, while simultaneously encouraging her children Lincoln and Harriet to color outside the lines.

www.ingramcontent.com/pod-product-compliance
Lightning Source LLC
Chambersburg PA
CBHW020436220526
45464CB00002B/730